Exploring the Mennonite Hymnal: Essays

Mary Oyer

Worship Series No. 7a

FAITH AND LIFE PRESS
Newton, Kansas

MENNONITE PUBLISHING HOUSE
Scottdale, Pennsylvania

Library of Congress Number 80-70825
ISBN 0-87303-044-3
Printed in the United States of America
Copyright © 1980 by Faith and Life Press, Newton, Kansas 67114 and Mennonite
Publishing House, Scottdale, Pennsylvania 15683

Table of Contents

Preface

Ten years ago this month *The Mennonite Hymnal* came off the press. Not long after that I began a series of visits to Mennonite congregations to introduce the book. In the process, I have been introduced to the church in surprising and rewarding ways. I have found a remarkable willingness to accept new hymns and new ways of singing the familiar, a willingness to live with the loss of favorites from past books and to expend energy on learning to sing the new.

The essays in this book grow directly out of those visits, and they are dedicated gratefully to the many people who have contributed to my experience of hymn singing in the life of the church.

Each essay begins with one hymn and proceeds through a series of associations or tangents. Essays might have tackled instead broad subjects of historical, aesthetic, or practical character—the German chorale in Mennonite books, perhaps, or the contribution of the music to the meaning of the hymn, or how to choose a good tempo for congregational singing. The book might have been neater and more orderly with such an organization.

The idea of using a hymn as a point of departure for exploration came from the speaking style that gradually emerged through these years of visits to congregations. But it also reached back further to the preparation of *The Mennonite Hymnal*. I spent a sabbatical year (1963-64) in Edinburgh, Scotland, searching for the original form of the text and tune of each hymn, under the expert guidance of Erik Routley. It was always a joy to find what I was looking for, but I became more and more interested in the excursions away from the subject—the tangential material that enriched both the search and the discovery.

In this same manner, therefore, one hymn at a time, I have tried to present a few of the many facets inherent in each. For example, in describing *MH* 284, "As the Hart with Eager Yearning," GENEVA 42, I have dealt with these topics:

1. the unique character of French Calvinist psalm singing
2. the people who made the versified psalms, in French, and both German and English translations
3. sources of the tunes for the Calvinist psalms—Genevan tunes
4. the use of Calvinist psalms in American Mennonite books
5. the varied meters of the nine Genevan psalms in *The Mennonite Hymnal*
6. editorial decisions in notating the music
7. how to sing Genevan psalms with greater ease
8. the use of GENEVA 42 in larger musical works

There are references backward and forward within the series of essays. Aside from the essential details of author and composer, there is no uniformity in the topics chosen.

With the use of the Index, readers can piece together information on larger topics, such as metrical psalms, Mennonite hymnbooks, the life and works of a few composers and authors (Isaac Watts, Charles Wesley, Lowell Mason, for example), the ways music "speaks" in a hymn, and secular sources for tunes.

Each essay is somewhat dependent on those that precede it, so the book will function better read from beginning to end than used as a dictionary. I hope that it will suggest to readers how the brief annotations on hymns and tunes of the second and third books in this series can serve as points of departure for endless exploration.

I acknowledge gratefully the skill and care of the late J. P. Classen, John Ruth, and George Wiebe in collecting important data on texts and tunes during the preparation of *The Mennonite Hymnal* in the 1960s. And I appreciate deeply the counsel of Miriam Lind, Dorothy McCammon, Harold Moyer, Ellen Jane Lorenz Porter, Orlando Schmidt, Anita Stoltzfus, George and Esther Wiebe, and my family—Verna, John, and Kathryn—during the writing of the present book. Each one helped in some way to shape its final form.

Mary Oyer

Using the Mennonite Hymnal

Material at the Head

To explore the function of the various parts of *The Mennonite Hymnal* let us look in detail at one hymn, *MH* 170, "Alas and Did My Savior Bleed."

The material at the head of each hymn can be useful in a variety of ways. The large print in *MH* 170, for example, identifies the text quickly by presenting its first line and *The Mennonite Hymnal* number.

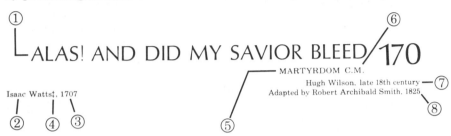

The small print is easily ignored. However, the singer can find it rewarding to stop and observe each name, word, or symbol. The left side, which always concerns the text, indicates that Isaac Watts② is the author. We must go elsewhere to learn his birth and death dates, his nationality, and his religious beliefs. The date,③ 1707, is that of the first publication of the text, although for some hymns in this book the year of the actual writing is given instead. (The distinction between the two is not made.) The date 1707 is informative in a general way because it suggests a kind of imagery and use of language quite different from that of other eras—the Reformation or the 1930s, for example.

The sign, ‡④, after the author's name tells us that the compilers altered the original text beyond a single word (which would be shown by †). The editorial practice for *MH* 1969 was one of respect for the author's text unless, for reasons of clarity or theological position, a change seemed necessary. (There has been a shift since 1969 in the direction of extensive alterations to eliminate racist and sexist language from Christian worship.) There is no indication here of the reasons for altering "Alas and Did My Savior Bleed" nor of the specific word changes. For that kind of detail as well as further information on Isaac Watts, see pages 11 to 14.

The word *MARTYRDOM* in capital letters immediately beneath the title,⑤ is the name of the tune. Tune names are strange and interesting and often reveal something about the place or circumstances of the composition. However, none of that background appears on this page. MARTYRDOM is simply the identification for the tune.

C.M.⑥ is the abbreviation for common meter, the label for the meter of the poem, 8.6.8.6. It counts the number of syllables for each line of the text, not the number of musical notes:

```
 1    2    3    4    5    6    7    8
 A - las! and  did  my   Sav - ior bleed?
   1    2    3    4        5    6
 And  did  my  Sov - ereign die?
```

Another 8 and 6 follow to make the complete stanza. The designation C.M. can help one choose, through the Metrical Index on page 617 of *The Mennonite Hymnal,* an alternate common meter tune for the text.

Further information on the tune appears below the tune name. In this case only a general time period is known for the tune, which Hugh Wilson⑦ composed. The particular arrangement⑧ by Robert Archibald Smith can be dated, 1825. Pages 14 and 15 spell out additional details.

Indexes

Another rich source of information in a hymnal is, of course, its indexes. The index at the very end of *The Mennonite Hymnal,* which is by its placement the most accessible, leads us to the proper page by the first line of the hymn. But the six additional indexes help us to use the hymnal more fully and imaginatively. The Topical Index and the Index of Scriptural Allusions are by nature flexible and expandable. They can never be completed or closed. Users of *The Mennonite Hymnal* could develop either index to fill their own particular needs.

"Alas and Did My Savior Bleed," *MH* 170, appears in the Topical Index under Communion, Consecration, and Jesus Christ (Priesthood). One could possibly place it also under Confession, Grace, or Jesus Christ (Suffering of). In any case the Index could be expanded. An entry such as Reformation Day could incorporate the three Anabaptist hymns—*MH* 40, 344, and 384—and further hymns and tunes of the 1520s and 30s—*MH* 38, 173, and 234, for example.

The Index of Scriptural Allusions includes *MH* 170 under Isaiah 53:5, Matthew 27:45 and 2 Corinthians 5:21, but any individual can make further connections with the Bible.

The first Index of Tunes, Alphabetical, shows us at once that MARTYRDOM is found elsewhere in *The Mennonite Hymnal* at number 285. There it is combined with a late seventeenth-century versification of Psalm 42. Thus MARTYRDOM functions as a "common tune," a vehicle for differing subjects and emphases.

Metrical Index

We can find MARTYRDOM① in the Metrical Index of Tunes through the meter, C.M., p. 617 (Fig. 1). If we had forgotten the name but wanted to find the tune, we could trace it through its meter, though in the case of a common-meter tune the process could be long. There are fifty-seven common-meter tunes. This index suggests tunes to substitute for the one

SHORT METER (2)
S.M. 6.6.8.6.

Bellwoods, 88
Benjamin, 176
Boylston, 350
Dennis, 385
Ferguson, 351
Festal Song, 441
Franconia, 279, 500
Gerar, 382
Golden Hill, 419
Laban, 321
Mornington, 214
St. Bride, 340
St. Michael, 301, 507
St. Thomas, 245
Schumann, 364
Silver Street, 330
Southwell, 246, 255
Sweet Day, 66
Trentham, 216

SHORT METER
with Refrain

Marion, 277
Welcome Voice, 549
We're Marching to Zion, 529

SHORT METER DOUBLE
S.M.D. 6.6.8.6. D.

Bealoth, 380
Diademata, 191, 449
Terra Beata, 49

COMMON METER (3)
C.M. 8.6.8.6.

Abbey, 302
Abridge, 82, 145
Antioch, 122
Arlington, 348, 499
Azmon, 104
Bromsgrove, 515
Byefield, 239
Cheshire, 241
Christmas, 138, 332
Coleshill, 371
Consolation, 256
Coronation, 95
Crimond, 67
Dedham, 282, 383
Diadem, 601
Dundee, 258, 290, 394
Dunfermline, 47, 80, 278, 402
Eden, 275
Elizabethtown, 305
Evan, 259
Geneva, 74
Glenluce, 299
Goshen, 438
Gratitude, 479
Green Hill, 451
Irish, 41

Kilmarnock, 283
King's Langley, 513
Land of Rest, 370
Lobt Gott, ihr Christen, 136, 250
Love's Consecration, 411
Maitland, 345
Martyrdom, 170, 285 ◄── (1)
Meditation, 473
Naomi, 213, 336
Nativity, 368
Newbold, 105
Nun danket all', 223
Ortonville, 187
Richmond, 32, 149, 501
St. Agnes, 108, 461
St. Anne, 84, 378
St. Flavian, 315, 400
St. Magnus, 81, 189
St. Martin's, 109
St. Peter, 102, 387
St. Stephen, 288
Salzburg, 83
Serenity, 150
Shaddick, 297
Solon, 242
Tallis' Ordinal, 28, 422
Warwick, 482
Wetherby, 157
Winchester Old, 268, 393
Windsor, 46, 320
Zerah, 125

COMMON METER
with Refrain

Bound for the Promised Land, 294
Christ Liveth in Me, 568
El Nathan, 586
God Cares, 574
Stockton, 553

COMMON METER DOUBLE
C.M.D. 8.6.8.6. D.

Bethlehem, 458
Bonar, 232
Carol, 126
Communion, 112
Ellacombe, 50, 155, 410
Kingsfold, 231
Release, 218
Resignation, 63
St. Matthew, 152
St. Michel's, 196

COMMON METER DOUBLE
with Refrain

Faith Is the Victory, 589

LONG METER (4)
L.M. 8.8.8.8.

Alfreton, 64
Alstone, 421
Angelus, 309, 494

Figure 1, p. 617

printed in *The Mennonite Hymnal.* One could try "Alas, and Did My Savior Bleed" with many other tunes. Some, like ST. MARTIN'S, CORONATION, and ANTIOCH, would suit metrically but would express too much exuberance for the text. ST. AGNES and SOLON might work better, or one could use some of the historic common tunes for psalms—DUNDEE, DUNFERMLINE, or WINCHESTER OLD. With a little study, a Metrical Index of Tunes makes many texts immediately accessible to a congregation.

The Metrical Index begins with the most typical meters in the English language—②Short Meter, ③Common Meter, and ④Long Meter, each of which is doubled in length also (Fig. 1). Then meters are presented in numerical order, beginning with the shortest first line, four syllables (Fig. 2) and ending with the longest, 14 syllables (Fig. 3).

4.6.6.4.6.6.9.9.4.
Gott ist getreu, 85
5.5.5.5.
Hubbard, 339
5.5.5.5.6.5.6.5.
Old 104th, 596
5.5.7.D.5.5.5.5.9. D.
In Dir ist Freude, 90
5.5.8.8.5.5.
Seelenbräutigam, 319
5.6.8.5.5.8.
Crusaders' Hymn, 97
6.4.6.4. with Refrain
Need, 578
6.4.6.4. D.
Bread of Life, 222
Doane, 96

Figure 2, p. 618

Ihr Kinderlein, kommet, 470
St. Denio, 43, 474
Towner, 580
11.11.11.11. with Refrain
To God Be the Glory, 532
Whiter Than Snow, 583
11.12.12.10.
Nicaea, 5
12.10.12.10.
Was lebet, was schwebet, 139
12.11.12.11.
Kremser, 12
12.12. with Refrain
Hallelujah, 'tis Done, 537
12.12.12.7. with Refrain
Christ Returneth, 570
14.14.4.7.8.
Lobe den Herren, 9

Figure 3, p. 620

Many of the German tunes and gospel songs in *The Mennonite Hymnal* have unique metrical patterns which do not allow for substituting tunes.

Continuing to move backward in the hymnal, we find the Index of Composers, Arrangers, and Sources. Hugh Wilson and Robert Archibald Smith are each represented by only one tune, which, as we have seen, is used twice.

In contrast, Isaac Watts's name needs a good deal of space in the Index of Authors, Translators, and Sources. Thirty-seven hymns are listed (Fig. 4), though numbers 165 and 167 are the same text with different tunes. The author's life span, 1674-1748, is given as well. A reading of all thirty-six hymns would give one a quick but helpful view of Watts's world and his attitude toward God.

Wagner, Jorg (d. 1527), 344
Walther, Johann (1496-1570), 195
Walworth, Clarence Augustus (1820-1900), 1
Wardlaw, Ralph (1779-1853), 286
Ware, Henry (1794-1843), 175, 461
Waring, Anna Laetita (1823-1910), 252
Warner, Anna Bartlett (1820-1915), 303
Watt, Lauchlan MacLean (1867-1957), 353
Watts, Isaac (1674-1748), 18, 19, 25, 34, 35, 36, 39,
46, 48, 50, 63, 66, 72, 79, 81, 84, 105, 109, 122,
147, 165, 167, 170, 203, 220, 245, 315, 326, 327,
348, 382, 392, 499, 507, 515, 529, 623
Webb, Benjamin (1820-1885), 190
Webster, Bradford Gray (1954), 616

Figure 4, p. 614

10

That is the extent of the indexes in *The Mennonite Hymnal*. But still others are possible. The church musician or minister could construct further arrangements to facilitate the use of this hymnal.

Using Other Sources

"Alas and Did My Savior Bleed," *MH* 170, has served as the illustrative hymn and tune for looking at the information given with the hymn and in the indexes in *The Mennonite Hymnal.*

If we want to find further accurate and detailed material on texts, John Julian's *Dictionary of Hymnology* would be the first place to look. This book, published in 1892 with a supplement of 247 pages in 1907, consists of 1768 pages of fine print. Under the title, "Alas and Did My Savior Bleed," page 34, in alphabetical order among the A's, the first six lines read:

I. Watts. [Passiontide.] 1st pub. in the 1st ed. of his *Hymns and Spiritual Songs,* 1707 and again in the enlarged ed. of the same 1709, Bk. ii., No. 9, in 6 st. of 4 1., and entitled "Godly sorrow arising from the Sufferings of Christ."

Thirteen more lines give a brief history of the hymn's use, suggesting that certain alterations are made.

From pages 1236 to 1241 we find the article on "Watts, Isaac." It begins, "The father of Dr. Watts was a respected Nonconformist, and at the birth of the child, and during its infancy, twice suffered imprisonment for his religious convictions." (That may explain, incidentally, the remarkable attraction Mennonites feel for Watts. His nonconformist, anti-state-church views create a special affinity. *The Mennonite Hymnal* has more texts by Watts than by any other author.) Watt's birth and death facts are given: July 17, 1674, Southampton, England, to November 25, 1748, Stoke Newington, along with details about his education, occupation, and writings.

Julian lists 454 hymns and versions of psalms by Watts which were in common use in his day—late nineteenth century. However, hymns and psalms of greater importance appear alphabetically by first line in the dictionary. The index shows that Watts appears on 155 additional pages and 18 more in the supplement. Julian's *Dictionary of Hymnology* is so valuable, even though it is almost one hundred years old (incidentally, most of our hymns are over one hundred years old), that every congregation should consider buying the two-volume reprint for the church library.

Two works stand out in the list of Watts's publications—*Hymns and Spiritual Songs,* 1707, and *The Psalms of David,* 1719. Most of his poems in *The Mennonite Hymnal* come from these two sources, so that the dates 1707 and 1719 at the head of a hymn are informative in a specific way.

A second major source for learning about hymns is the handbook or companion to a hymnal. Lester Hostetler's *Handbook to the Mennonite*

11

Hymnary, 1949, [1] has such a relationship to the 1940 *Mennonite Hymnary* of the General Conference Mennonite Church. It is the only companion to a Mennonite hymnal until this present book. Hostetler's work represents the first movement away from the exclusive use of hymn singing as a folk tradition and toward self-consciousness about the material we use. It paved the way for a new attitude toward making a Mennonite hymnbook. *The Mennonite Hymnal,* 1969, is the first Mennonite hymnal for which the original texts and tunes were sought out (perhaps 90% were found) and considered seriously by the compilers.

Here is Lester Hostetler's entry on *MH* 170:

108. Alas! and did my Savior bleed   Isaac Watts, 1674-1748

A fine hymn of consecration, published by Watts in his *Hymns and Spiritual Songs,* 1707, under the title "Godly Sorrow Arising from the Sufferings of Christ." Dr. Charles S. Robinson states that "more conversions in Christian biography are credited to this hymn than to any other." Fanny Crosby, the blind poet, ten of whose lyrics are found in the *Hymnary,* credits this hymn with a share in her conversion. In telling the story she says that during a revival in the old Thirtieth Street Church, New York, in 1850, several times she sought the Savior at the altar; but not until one evening, November 20, did the light come. "After a prayer was offered they began to sing the good old consecration hymn, 'Alas! and did my Saviour bleed,' and when they had reached the third line of the fourth stanza, 'Here, Lord, I give myself away,' my very soul flooded with celestial light."

Handbook writers borrow heavily from Julian's *Dictionary of Hymnology* and from one another. The resources for handbooks become richer with each year. The bibliography on pages 15 and 16 presents some of the most recent and a few of the significant handbooks of past decades, from which many writers have borrowed extensively.

A few unusual hymnbooks include concise notes on the hymns and tunes within the books themselves. The *Hymnal for Colleges and Schools,* edited under the direction of E. Harold Geer, and published by Yale University Press in 1956, is such a work. My own interest in studying hymns and tunes began with those notes—only 51 pages; after that I discovered fuller handbooks.

The third and possibly best source for the study of a hymn is the original text itself. One might have to visit a large library to find it, but it is well worth the effort. Watts's poetry is more accessible than that of most authors of hymns. The complete *Hymns and Spiritual Songs* is published in a scholarly edition which shows the changes in the hymns between 1707 and 1748. (Selma Bishop, London: The Faith Press, 1962) Here one can read the complete "Alas and Did My Savior Bleed?" and even see how the editions changed during the first forty years of the hymn's life. *The Mennonite Hymnal* includes stanzas 1, 3, 4, and 6. Stanzas 2 and 5 read as follows in many of the early editions:

(brackets indicated that the stanza could be omitted.)

> Stanza 2:
> [The Body slain, sweet *Jesus,* thine,
>   And bath'd in its own Blood,
> While all expos'd to Wrath divine
>   The glorious Sufferer stood.]

> Stanza 5:
> Thus might I hide my blushing Face
>   While his dear Cross appears.
> Dissolve my Heart in Thankfulness,
>   And melt my Eyes to Tears.

In the remaining stanzas there are several phrases that have troubled Christians through the years. The first stanza ended, "For such a worm as I," using a cliché of the times to express humility. In stanza 3 Watts had written, "When God the mighty Maker died."

The following table shows what Mennonite editors did with these lines in past hymnals, and gives, incidentally, a complete list of Mennonite hymnals in English:

History of alterations in "Alas and Did my Savior Bleed?"
Version for underlined words given.
St. 1: For *such a worm* as I.
St. 3: When *God, the mighty Maker, died.*

Hymnal	St. of original used	St. 1	St.3
A Selection of Ps. Hymns & Sp. Songs (Mennonite Hymns) 1847 p. 70	All	such a worm	God the mighty Maker died
Hymns and Tunes 1890 No. 57	1,3,4,5,6	such a worm	Christ the glorious Savior died
Church and Sunday School Hymnal, 1902 No. 249 Supplement, 1911	1,3,4,5,6 with Refrain	such a worm	God's own Son was crucified
Life Songs No. 1 1916 No. 264	1,3,4,5,6	such a worm	God's own Son was crucified
Church Hymnal 1927 No. 315	1,3,4,5,6	such a worm	God's own Son was crucified
Life Songs No. 2 1938 No. 339	1,3,6	such a worm	(stanza omitted)
Songs of the Church 1953	(omitted)		

MENNONITE CHURCH

Mennonite Hymnal. A Blending of Many Voices 1894 No. 116	1,3,4,5,6	such a worm	God, the mighty Maker, died
Mennonite Hymn Book 1927 No. 101	1,3,4,5,6	such a one	Christ, the mighty Maker, died
Mennonite Hymnary 1940 No. 108	1,3,4,6	sinners such	Christ, the mighty Maker, died
The Youth Hymnary 1956	(omitted)		

Obviously, the page at *MH* 170 cannot show all these changes, but the sign, ‡, invites interested persons to see how hymn editors over the years have tried to deal with the theological problems the hymn raises. The Text Committee of *The Mennonite Hymnal* was working in the 1960s when the "God is dead" movement was vigorous. Watts's original stanza 3 had quite different associations in that context, so they chose "Christ, the mighty Maker, died."

There is nothing so complete as Julian's *Dictionary of Hymnology* for studying tunes. However, *Hymn Tune Names,* by Robert McCutcheon, (Abingdon, 1957), presents nearly one thousand tunes, indicating the meter and the pitch relationships of the first line. Then he gives the various names for the same tune. MARTYRDOM, on page 99 begins, "C.M. (3: S/d—L/S—dr/m—r/d—); Hugh Wilson, ca. 1800. Also called ALL SAINTS, AVON, BOSTAL, DRUMCLOG, FENWICK, INVERNESS." McCutcheon suggests probable reasons for each name. His Melodic Index helps the reader find a tune name from the syllables.

Katharine Smith Diehl's *Hymns and Tunes—An Index,* (Scarecrow Press, 1966) has a similar tune index. The author indicates in the section called *Tune Names* the fifty-three books (of seventy-eight) in which MARTYRDOM appears. (Her book also indexes composers, authors, and first lines of hymns.)

In addition we can find excellent information for certain categories of tunes:

1. Chorales. German Lutheran tunes. J. Zahn. *Die Melodien der Deutschen Evangelischen Kirchenlieder,* 6 volumes, 1889-93.
2. Genevan Psalm tunes, from Calvin's day. P. Pidoux. *Le Psautier Huguenot,* 2 volumes, 1962.
3. British Psalm tunes. M. Frost. *English and Scottish Psalm and Hymn Tunes, c. 1543-1677,* 1953.

And occasionally one composer's tunes are drawn together in a useful organization, such as in Henry L. Mason, *Hymn-Tunes of Lowell Mason,* 1944.

Frequently a hymnal handbook is a good source for tune study. The *Hymnal 1940 Companion,* 1949 (Episcopal), one of the best American handbooks, served as a model for later books. It describes MARTYRDOM thus:

> The . . . tune, *Martyrdom, Fenwick, or Drumclog,* by Hugh Wilson, was originally in duple time and appeared as a broadside with but melody and bass. Its publication by Robert A. Smith in *Sacred Music Sung at St. George's Church, Edinburgh,* 1825, in triple time, has led the tune to be frequently attributed to Smith. In fact, Wilson's heirs brought suit and proved their rights in court. It has been suggested that Smith mistook the name *Fenwick* for that of the martyred Covenanter, James Fenwick, and so rechristened it with its present name. Anne G. Gilchrist, in *The Choir* (London), XXV (1934), 155-6, raises the interesting question as to whether or not *Martyrdom* was originally the tune of a Scotch ballad. (p. 259)

[1] This handbook, which is out of print, is available on loan from the libraries of Mennonite colleges.

A Bibliography of Basic Sources

There are two societies devoted to hymnody:
The Hymn Society of America
W. Thomas Smith, Executive Director
Wittenberg University
Springfield, Ohio 45501

Hymn Society of Great Britain and Ireland
John Wilson, Treasurer
30 East Meads
Guildford, Surrey GU2 5SP
England

The Hymn Society of America publishes *The Hymn* quarterly and a series, *Papers of the Hymn Society of America,* on various hymnological subjects. Membership is $15.00 a year. *The Bulletin of the Hymn Society of Great Britain and Ireland* comes with the annual fee—$8.00 in the U.S.A. and $9.50 in Canada.

The Hymn Society of America published a useful bibliography of 25 pages in 1964, *A Short Bibliography for the Study of Hymns,* with a revision and updating by Keith C. Clark, *A Selective Bibliography for the Study of Hymns 1980.*

Handbooks to hymnals give a great deal of information. (See descriptions of the *Handbook to the Mennonite Hymnary* on pages 12 and 110-11.) The following four American handbooks would be especially useful for church libraries:

Episcopal: *The Hymnal 1940 Companion.* New York: Church Hymnal Corporation, 1949.

United Church: Ronander, Albert C. and Ethel K. Porter. *Guide to the Pilgrim Hymnal* (1958). Philadelphia: United Church Press, 1966.

Methodist: Gealy, Fred D., Austin C. Lovelace, and Carlton R. Young. *Companion to the Hymnal* (1964). Nashville: Abingdon Press, 1970.

Baptist: Reynolds, William J. *Companion to Baptist Hymnal* (1975). Nashville: Broadman Press, 1976.

Handbooks for British and German hymnals appear in footnotes throughout this book. "A Bibliography of Handbooks and Companions to Hymnals: American, Canadian, and English," by Keith C. Clark is published in four parts in *The Hymn,* beginning with the July 1979 issue (volume 30, number 3).

A few other basic sources:

John Julian. *A Dictionary of Hymnology Setting forth the Origin and History of Christian Hymns of All Ages and Nations.* London: J. Murray, 1892-1907, and reprint, New York: Dover Publications, 1957.

An extensive dictionary of American hymns is being prepared by Leonard Ellinwood, assisted by Elizabeth Lockwood: *Dictionary of American Hymnology,* 7811 Custer Road, Bethesda, Maryland 20014.

Benson, Louis F. *The English Hymn: Its Development and Use in Worship.* New York: George H. Doran Co., 1915. Reprint: Richmond: John Knox Press, 1962.

Blume, Friedrick. *Protestant Church Music: A History.* Second edition, translated from German. New York: W. W. Norton, 1974.

Ellinwood, Leonard. *History of American Church Music.* New York: Morehouse-Gorham Company, 1953.

Foote, Henry W. *Three Centuries of American Hymnody.* Cambridge: Harvard University Press, 1940. Reprint: Hamden, Conn.: The Shoe String Press, 1961.

Routley, Erik. *The Music of Christian Hymnody.* London: Independent Press, 1957.

51 and 52. All Creatures of Our God and King. LASST UNS ERFREUEN

Occasionally religious revivals produce songs in a new popular idiom. Psalm tunes in ballad meter (8.6.8.6., *MH* 28, 393, for example) and German vernacular hymns (*MH* 325, 611) appeared early in the sixteenth-century Reformation. The gospel song of the Moody-Sankey revivals reflected popular songs of America around 1875 (*MH* 563, 573). Hymnody in the 1960s and 70s borrows readily from secular sources.

The *lauda* (plural, *laude*) was a popular religious song that emerged in the revival under the influence of St. Francis of Assisi (1182-1226) and extended into the fourteenth century. At a time when Latin was the universal religious language, sacred *laude* in Italian were the vehicles of praise for wandering pilgrims seeking penance.

St. Francis's *Canticle of the Sun* is a *lauda* whose music has been lost. The paraphrase, "All Creatures of Our God and King," by an English clergyman, William Henry Draper (1855-1933), follows the broad outline of the text. For comparison, here is a more direct prose translation of the material we find in stanza 3:

Be Thou praised, my Lord, of Sister Water,
  which is much useful and humble and precious and pure.

Be Thou praised, my Lord, of Brother Fire,
  by which Thou hast lightened the night,
  and he is beautiful and joyful and robust and strong.
      (Robert Steele, *Little Flowers,* p. 388)

The Mennonite Hymnal omits two stanzas of Draper's paraphrase:

4. Dear mother earth, who day by day
   Untoldest blessings on our way,
     O praise him, alleluia!
   The flowers and fruits that in thee grow
   Let them his glory also show;
     O praise him . . .

6. And thou, most kind and gentle death,
   Waiting to hush our latest breath,
     O praise him, alleluia!
   Thou leadest home the child of God,
   And Christ our Lord the way hath trod;
     O praise him . . .

The tune appeared in two distinct arrangements in the seventeenth century. The earlier form (*MH* 52) alternated a phrase of the text with the refrain, "Alleluia" or "O praise him!" (For the use of Alleluia refrains, see also *MH* 61, 62, 179, 618.) The second form (*MH* 51) grouped phrases in pairs. It appeared in the *English Hymnal,* 1906, with the text, "Ye watchers and ye holy ones." (*Life Songs 2,* 21.) The distinguished musical editor of that hymnal was Ralph Vaughan Williams (1872-1958). His arrangement of the tune is fairly thick in texture, sometimes including five parts rather than strictly four. The directions in the *English Hymnal* call for unison singing except in the refrains, where the choir presumably joins the organ to provide harmony.

It may be useful for part-singing Mennonites to know Vaughan Williams's views on congregational singing. In the Preface to the *English Hymnal,* after explaining various uses of unison singing and organ accompaniment, he said, "In any case the congregation must *always* sing the melody, and the *melody only.*" (p. xiii) This view decidedly sets Mennonite tradition apart from that of the Church of England and may explain why we find Vaughan Williams's hymns relatively difficult for our styles of singing. His own compositions—*MH* 210, 395, 503, and his arrangements—71, 94, 115, 231, 304, 457, and 513— probably come off better with the support of an instrument.

230. Art Thou Weary, Art Thou Languid?
STEPHANOS

Hymns are generally in strophic form—that is, each stanza maintains the same meter so that a tune which suits the first stanza will fit the remaining stanzas. "Art Thou Weary" has an unusual meter of 8.5.8.3. The organization within each stanza is unique also. A dialogue or conversation takes place. Each stanza begins with a question which is answered in the last half. (See *MH* 271 for a similar structure.)

Albert Baily imagines the dramatic scene, set in the context out of which John Mason Neale's text grew. Stephen, the Sabaite, (c. 725-94) joined a monastery of the Eastern Church in the Kidron Valley near Jerusalem when he was a young man. Bailey sees Stephen, troubled by the political and religious unrest of the time, asking fundamental questions about his faith. Bailey describes the poem as " 'the call to religious life' or more accurately 'the monastic life.' "[1] A wise elder monk asks the first question and answers Stephen's following questions. The seventh and last verse is not included in *The Mennonite Hymnal:*

Finding, following, keeping, struggling,
　Is He sure to bless?
"Angels, Martyrs, Prophets, Virgins
　Answer, Yes!"[2]

In many hymnals the word "languid" has been replaced by words such as "troubled" and "heavy-laden," but the Text Committee chose the original wording. They changed one word, however (indicated by † after the author's name). In stanza 4 "portion" replaces the original "guerdon."

John Mason Neale (1818-66) was a part of the Oxford Movement, in which Anglicans from 1833 onward studied pre-Reformation Catholicism and revived some of its literature and liturgy. Neale combined excellent scholarship in Greek and Latin with a fine poetic sense to produce translations of early Christian hymns which are still in general use. (Latin: *MH* 92, 111, 154, 373, 416, 610; Greek: 174, 178.) "Art Thou Weary" first appeared as a translation of a hymn by Stephen the Sabaite in *Hymns of the Eastern Church*. However, in a later edition, Neale indicated that his poem included so little from Stephen that it was essentially an original work.

Hymns Ancient and Modern, 1861, was the outstanding hymnal growing out of the Oxford Movement. Henry Williams Baker (1821-77) led the movement to publish a combination of old Latin texts with their Gregorian chants (such as *MH* 92 and 404) and new texts by leaders of the Oxford Movement (for example, *MH* 221, 454, 518 by Baker; 279, 483, 491 by Keble; 316 by Newman). A new kind of hymn tune—faster and more regular than previous tunes—emerged as well (Examples: *MH* 5, 495). Baker wrote the tune STEPHANOS, meaning diadem in Greek, for the 1868 expansion of *Hymns Ancient and Modern*.

The text is in clear questions and answers. The tune, STEPHANOS, is also paired in psychological question-answer or statement-response relationships. The music of a hymn often "speaks" in this way. One could look at this procedure as a cliché, obvious and overused. But it is also a fundamental and universal principle derived from nature and human relationships. It symbolizes the back-and-forth or complementing motions in nature—walking left and right, breathing in and out, life and death, day and night. It matches conversational patterns and human exchanges. It is so basic a principle that it permeates other cultures as well. For example probably the most common musical pattern in Black Africa is call-and-response, solo answered by group. Symmetry in visual design is the ideal of many traditional African sculptors—one side of the sculpture "speaks" clearly to the other. In Chinese philosophy, the complementing pair of opposites—*yin* and *yang*—unite harmoniously.

The Oriental symbol presents visually the opposites joined into one.

In the Bible there are many opposites which unite to present the whole reality. The description of Creation in Genesis is of pairs of opposites: light and darkness, day and night, land and sea, male and female. The Old and New Testaments yield innumerable correspondences. Liturgies are also based on complementing opposites—fixed and changing texts, fixed and movable feasts, action toward God and from God.

I believe that Mennonites fulfill a fundamental need for symbolizing through singing. Thus, "meaning" in a hymn extends far beyond words.

[1] Albert Bailey, *The Gospel in Hymns.* New York: Charles Scribners, 1950, p. 290.

[2] John Mason Neale, *Hymns of the Eastern Church,* 4th ed. London: J. T. Hayes, 1882, p. 146.

22. Let All the World. LUCKINGTON.

"Let All the World in Ev'ry Corner Sing" is one of three remarkable poems in *The Mennonite Hymnal* by George Herbert (1593-1632). His collection of poems, *The Temple: Sacred Poems and Private Ejaculations,* was published in 1633, the year after his death. One reason they were "private" rather than public worship pieces lies in the exclusive use of psalms or other Scriptures in the English church of his day. The efforts of George Wither during the previous decade to publish his freely-composed hymns, with tunes by Orlando Gibbons, had failed completely.

But many of the poems were "private" also because their meters were unusual. Psalm tunes were overwhelmingly common meter (C.M. 8.6.8.6., ballad meter) (see pp. 7-10), long meter (L.M.8.8.8.8.), or short meter (S.M.6.6.8.6.). "Let All the World" has a 10.4. chorus and a 6.6.6.6. verse. Figure 5 is a facsimile of the text from the 1633 edition. An antiphon is a refrain-like device framing the verses.

John Wesley was fond of Herbert's poems, but he rearranged a number of them to fit the regular-meter tunes of the eighteenth century.

Basil Harwood (1859-1949) in LUCKINGTON, repeated the chorus at the beginning of the second verse. In 1911 Ralph Vaughan Williams made a setting for baritone solo, chorus, and orchestra which follows Herbert's antiphon plan explicitly. It is sometimes arranged for congregational singing, but most hymn tunes follow Harwood's plan.

Harwood called for antiphonal singing in the verses, where the music is repeated in pairs. Architecturally the divided chancel divides choir members into two groups facing each other. Psalms are presented regularly in antiphonal form in the Anglican church, and this hymn lends itself to such question-answer procedure as well. Mennonite congregations can sing this tune antiphonally when the music is familiar.

¶ Antiphon.

Cho. Let all the world in ev'ry corner fing,
 My God and King.

 Vers. The heav'ns are not too high,
 His praife may thither flie:
 The earth is not too low ,
 His praifes there may grow.

Cho. Let all the world in ev'ry corner fing,
 My God and King.

 Vers. The church with pfalms muft fhout.
 No doore can keep them out:
 But above all, the heart
 Muft bear the longeft part.

Cho. Let all the world in ev'ry corner fing,
 My God and King.

Figure 5

The Temple: Sacred Poems and Private Ejaculations.
George Herbert.
Facsimile reprint of first edition, 1633.
London: Elliot Stock, 62 Paternoster Row, [n.d.]

LUCKINGTON looks dull on its page in *The Mennonite Hymnal*. The committee had hoped to change the whole and half notes to halves and quarters. Such a change would make no genuine change in tempo, but the psychological difference would be helpful to congregations. However, the owners of the copyright insisted that it remain exactly as it first appeared in the *Oxford Hymn Book, 1908,* of which the composer was the musical advisor to the editors. Perhaps they wanted any further uses of the hymn to remain as close as possible to the lovely appearance of each page of the *Oxford Hymn Book*, which was printed in Walpergen type (see Fig. 10, p. 52), introduced by the *Yattendon Hymnal* in 1899.

How then can we find an appropriate tempo for a hymn? The duration of notes does not help us; this is not a slow hymn because of the many whole notes. Words do help, but they are not as reliable as the internal indicators of the music. We can look for these general signs:

1. How much variety of note values is present? Here we had only ♩, ○ and ○·, with frequent repetitions, pointing us to a faster tempo.

2. How do individual parts move? Here the soprano and bass parts leap vigorously, causing us to slow down more than the rhythm would suggest.

3. How complicated is the harmony? We can tell in part by the movement in the bass. Singing only *doh* and *sol* (as in many gospel songs) simplifies and speeds the movement. But here there is complexity. We notice that every melody note has a change of chord. Complexity slows the tempo.

4. How do the phrases shape up? Is the tempo fast enough to complete a phrase in a breath span?

These indicators offer no absolutes, but they are useful guides to organists and song leaders. In addition, the size of the singing group and the acoustics of the room present external influences on tempo which should be considered for each specific occasion.

The two other poems by Herbert in *The Mennonite Hymnal* are cast in standard meters. *MH* 301 is in short meter. We need regularity in order to cope with its complex thought. Herbert's title is "The Elixer"—that substance used by the medieval alchemist to turn baser materials to gold. That image is needed to make the "tincture 'For Thy sake' " come through with transforming power.

MH 445 is in 7.7.7.7. meter. We could have simplified its use by organizing it with a $\frac{2}{2}$ time signature:

It is too valuable a hymn to be lost because of its forbidding appearance on the page.

479. I Owe the Lord a Morning Song.
GRATITUDE

"I Owe the Lord a Morning Song" first appeared in *Hymns and Tunes, for Public and Private Worship and Sunday Schools,* published in 1890 (Fig. 6). Amos Herr (1816-97), a Lancaster County preacher and advocate of the use of English in worship, wrote the text. Unable to get to church on one snowy Sunday morning, he praised God with a new text. *Hymns and Tunes* indicates that GRATITUDE was written by the committee; at any rate no one claimed the sole responsibility. The *Church and Sunday School Hymnal* of 1902 credited *Hymns and Tunes* with the music. The editors of the *Church Hymnal,* 1927, inserted Amos Herr's name for both text and tune, an attribution continued in *The Mennonite Hymnal,* 1969.

This might be called a typical (Old) Mennonite hymn. Its language is simple, straightforward, and functional, presenting abstractions rather than concrete images. Like most pre-electricity morning songs, the text expresses relief that the night has passed and uses day and light as symbols for enlightenment and heaven.

GRATITUDE, set in Aikin's seven shapes or character notes for easy reading, would have been a fine, simple song for singing schools. The bass part is limited to four notes. The sopranos cover one octave, but the inner voices use only five and six notes. Yet the simplicity does not mean dullness; the tune wears well.

In its simple way GRATITUDE makes a kind of journey and a return home again.[1] It does so with its question and answer phrases and its key signature. The first phrase is answered rather inconclusively by the second, which moves to a new key. The third phrase begins again with a slightly different question which is answered decisively this time. The key changes are standard for a short hymn, but they contribute to the "journey." The first half of the music adds one sharp to the sharp of the signature. The second half cancels the sharp of the signature with the natural (♮). Thus in a brief time we make a balanced excursion around the

---

[1] Departure and return form a universal psychological experience in myths and stories, and music can express it without use of words. Joseph Campbell, in *The Hero with a Thousand Faces* (Princeton: Princeton University Press, 1949, p. 30) describes its significance:

The standard path of the mythological adventure of the hero is a magnification of the formula represented in the rites of passage: *separation-initiation-return:* which might be named the nuclear unit of the monomyth. [The word is from James Joyce, *Finnegans Wake,* he says in a footnote.]

A hero ventures forth from the world of common day into a region of supernatural wonder: fabulous forces are there encountered and a decisive victory is won: the hero comes back from this mysterious adventure with the power to bestow boons on his fellowman.

I will sing aloud of thy mercy in the morning.   Ps. 59: 16.   **C. M.**

Figure 6

Hymns and Tunes for Public and Private Worship, and Sunday Schools.
Elkhart: Mennonite Publishing Co., 1890, p. 122.

keynote (G), and we come to the end with a sense of having departed and come home again.

Hymns and Tunes, 1890, was the first hymnal of the Mennonite Church to include tunes with the texts; hence its name. Previous publications consisted of texts only, usable with a separate tune book or with tunes transmitted orally. In 1890 the General Conference Mennonite Church also published its first official hymnal in the New World—*Gesangbuch mit Noten.* The compilation attempted to unify the Swiss and South German congregations already settled in America and the Russian and Prussian congregations that came to America in the 1870s. A comparison of the two books helps one to understand both the ethnic distance between the Mennonite Church and the General Conference Mennonites, and the richness of resources available when the two groups joined to produce *The Mennonite Hymnal,* 1969. Notice, for example, that *Hymns and Tunes* has only one third as many poetic meters as *Gesangbuch mit Noten* has, and uses the standard English psalm meters many times. *Hymns and Tunes* has almost lost its German Reformation background, which is still strong in *Gesangbuch mit Noten.* In addition, when the Mennonite Church committee needed a hymn or tune, someone wrote it. The General Conference Mennonites, on the other hand, preserved their tradition faithfully.

Group	Mennonite Church	General Conference Mennonite Church
Place of Publication	Elkhart, Indiana	Berne, Indiana
Number of Hymns	457	600
Number of Tunes	220	223
Language	English	German
Organization of Book	27 topics (diverse) arranged alphabetically	By creed or doctrine: Trinity, Scriptures, Christian Life, Times and Seasons

Number of meters (poetic)		35	109
Long meter	LM	39	8
Common meter	CM	60	8
Short meter	SM	25	1
Tunes:			
Number by Committee		19	0
Number by Mennonites		35	0
German tunes of 16th and 17th c.		2	30
American tunes by Mason, Bradbury, Hastings		39	11
American folk tunes		14	1
Gospel songs		c. 14	c. 5

55. God, the Lord Omnipotent. TOASIA

"God, the Lord Omnipotent" is one of six hymns and tunes in *The Mennonite Hymnal* from the non-Western world. (The others are: *MH* 209, 339, 362, 377, 498.) The committee had difficulty searching for songs from other cultures in the mid-1960s. Expressions in speech and music in non-Western idioms were hard to find because when hymns are translated into English and tunes are presented in Western notation, much of the uniqueness disappears.

The Taiwanese text of *MH* 55 translated by missionaries Boris and Clare Anderson, appeared in 1961 in the *E. A. C. C. Hymnal,* edited by D. T. Niles and published by the East Asian Christian Conference (Kyoto,

Japan). The preface points to the problem of linking Asian music to the English language: "The nature of the flow which belongs to much Asian music does not easily lend itself to English with its accents" (p. 1). Further, the Taiwanese would likely have enriched the unison melodies by adding a variety of instruments and complex rhythms.

The committee borrowed the melody of "God the Lord Omnipotent," omitting the occasional parts suggested in the *E. A. C. C. Hymnal.* Thus congregations who regularly sing in four parts can focus on the character of the melody. It is pentatonic (as are the other five Oriental songs in *The Mennonite Hymnal*). Here one can play all the notes on the five black keys of the piano beginning on E-flat. Unlike most Western hymn tunes, this one begins high and gradually descends. Its first half is similar to many ancient melodies which ethnomusicologists describe as cascading downward over a wide range.

A Taiwanese women's choir sang another text to TOASIA at the 1978 Mennonite World Conference. The editors of the *International Songbook,* Clarence Hiebert and Rosemary Wyse, had asked the Mennonite leaders of Taiwan for a suitable hymn to sing at the conference. They chose the tune TOASIA with the text used in their congregations. Here it is, versified by the editors:

1 Heav'n and earth, the day, the night,
   God created by his hand, his might,
   Twilight, darkness, dawn, and light.
   Perfect splendor, glorious the sight!

2 God is good; serve him with joy,
   He will bless, fear not, will not destroy,
   Clothing, shelter, all we eat,
   God prepares our ev'ry need to meet.

3 God is truth, is perfect light.
   Pray'r to idols leads you into night.
   They are made of wood and stone,
   Are not true; so trust in God alone.

4 God is infinitely great
   Saving sinners from their sin and fate,
   Pray to God, you will be heard;
   Nations, heed him, people trust his Word.

Excerpts from the letter accompanying the song, from J. N. (Han) Vandenberg, are enlightening:

   The hymn chosen by most of our Taiwan leaders here as an authentic Chinese melody and words is number 63 in the *Taiwanese Presbyterian Hymnal. . . .* This is the same melody which appears in *The Mennonite*

Hymnal #55. It is the Pe* Po or *Pepu hoan* melody. This indicates that it is a melody of the Plains aborigines of Taiwan who have been assimilated into the Chinese population and who do not exist as a distinct group anymore. Strains of this group are identifiable and always manifest a strong musical ability.

This hymn was chosen for its authentic Chinese melody, its typical 7.7.7.7. meter which is found in many Chinese songs and chants—often long narrations are given in this meter. The words (of anonymous authorship) express ideas which confront the Chinese Christian as he meditates on God's omnipotence and power in comparison to the legions of idols around him in his society. Some of these Chinese idioms are not altogether translatable.

Stanzas 5 and 6 of *MH* 55 appear beneath the staves. In contrast to the British preference for setting up the stanzas in poetic form for devotional reading, Mennonites follow the American custom of placing the text close to the music for ease of singing. Although our practice contributes to independent part singing, it makes us hesitate to fit syllables to a tune from this distance. This creation text needs all six stanzas. Stanza 5 carries on the flow of the creation story, and stanza 6 summarizes.

2 and 3. All People that on Earth Do Dwell. OLD HUNDREDTH

The earliest psalm text in *The Mennonite Hymnal* is "All People that on Earth Do Dwell." (The earliest English test is *MH* 645.) To participate in this metrical version the congregation must borrow the language of the past, fifty years before the publication of the King James Version of the Bible.

William Kethe (d. 1594), a Scot who fled to Geneva to escape the reign of Queen Mary of England, contributed this paraphrase of Psalm 100 to the *Anglo-Genevan Psalter,* 1561. He used the tune for Psalm 134 from the French Psalters of the time. The combination reached both the *Scottish Psalter* and an appendix to the *English Psalter* in 1564, and through the latter gained the name OLD HUNDREDTH, or the tune for the one hundreth Psalm in the Old Version.

Originally the text read, "Him serve with *fear*" in stanza 1 and "*The Lord ye know* is God" in stanza 2. The changes—"mirth" and "Know that the Lord" came with the *Scottish Psalter* of 1650. Julian, in the *Dictionary of Hymnology,* speculates that "flock" of stanza 2 may have been a printer's error early in the hymn's history. The original was "folk."

Louis Bourgeois (c.1510-c.1561), music editor for Calvin's Psalters, composed or arranged the tune for Psalm 134, and Claude Goudimel (c.1505-72), a composer of Roman Catholic liturgical music until his conversion to the Huguenot faith in 1558, made two complete settings in parts of the psalm tunes. The first, in 1564, was fairly ornate, with the melody usually in the soprano. He placed the psalm melody in the tenor for most of the simpler settings of 1565. (See Fig. 7 and *MH* 3.) In spite of their austerity, these settings did not seem to Goudimel suitable for worship in church. He indicated in a note to the reader that the addition of three parts is for praising God in the home; such activity, he said, should

Figure 7

Microfilm from Scottish National Library
  Edinburgh, Scotland
*Les Pseaumes mis en rime francoise, par Clement Marot et Theodore de Beze. Mis
  en musique a quatre parties par Claude Goudimel.*
Publ.: Francois Jaqui, 1565. Psalm 134.

not be viewed as wrong because the tune used with the psalm in church remains intact—clearly recognizable.

At about the same time, an Anabaptist treatise spoke more directly concerning the adornment that music might bring to a text. In his *Account of Our Religion, Doctrine and Faith,* 1545, Peter Riedemann (1505-56), a Hutterite bishop, missionary, and hymn writer, included a passage "Concerning Singing." Singing spiritual songs pleases God

if we sing in the right way, that is, attentively, in the fear of God and as inspired by the Spirit of Christ . . . [Songs] must . . . be sung as inspired by the same Spirit, if they are to be sung aright and to be of service to men.

Where this is not the case, and one singeth only for carnal joy or for the sweet sound or for some such reason, one misuseth them, changing them into what is carnal and worldly, and singeth not songs of the Spirit, but of the letter. Likewise also, he who enjoyeth listening for the music's sake—he heareth in the letter and not in the Spirit, so with him also is it without fruit; and because they are not used, sung and heard aright, he that so doeth sinneth greatly against God; for he useth his word, which was given for his salvation and as an urge to blessedness, as leading to the lust of the flesh and to sin. Thus, it is changed by him into harm, for though the song in itself is spiritual, yet is it to that man no longer a spiritual song. It is a worldly song, for it is not sung in the spirit.

He, however, who singeth in the Spirit, considereth diligently every word, how far and whither it goeth, why it hath been used and how it may serve to his betterment. . . .[1]

MH 3, Goudimel's version with the melody in the tenor (Fig. 7) is simple and straightforward, although its cadences are more complicated for the sopranos than in most hymns. *MH* 2 gives the melody as usual in the soprano, requiring that all the other parts be rearranged to some extent. Both of these forms retain the original rhythm, which stretches out the beginning of the last phrase in a surprising way. Two other versions are *MH* 638 and 639. *MH* 638 is the simplest form and probably the most familiar. *MH* 639 is like *MH* 2 except that all phrases present the same rhythm.

These four versions, moving as they do from the complexity of the original to the barest essentials of pitch and rhythm, point to the dilemma *The Mennonite Hymnal* Committee faced continually. Is the music of a hymn only a vehicle for words or does it have something unique to offer apart from words? The spirit of Peter Riedemann was with us often, as we chose the simplest and most functional music in order that worshipers could focus on the text.

But occasionally we chose a more difficult version for a congregation to sing "for carnal joy or for the sweet sound or for some such reason . . . for the music's sake." Sometimes we were convinced that something important could happen to the congregation through the music as well as the text, through nonverbal expression as well as words. The Spirit works in many ways. Rather than presenting a range of versions for a tune, as here with OLD HUNDREDTH, we sometimes gave two tunes for a text—one simple and the other difficult: *MH* 236 and 237, 232 and 231, 424 and 425, 430 and 432, for example. Although the words are the same for each pair, the music alters their meaning considerably in each case.

Two other versions of Psalm 100 appear in *The Mennonite Hymnal.* Isaac Watt's Long Meter original began:

1 Sing to the Lord with joyful voice;
  Let ev'ry land his name adore;
  The British Isles shall send the noise
  Across the ocean to the shore.

2 Nations, attend before his throne
  With solemn fear, with sacred joy
  Know that the Lord . . .

MH 48 is John Wesley's altered version, omitting the first stanza altogether and rewriting the beginning of the second.

MH 618 is a modern version of Psalm 100 (Psalm 99 in Roman Catholic numbering) by Joseph Gelineau, a French priest who wanted to make psalm singing available to congregations. His Psalm 100 forms the subject for the next essay.

[1] Bungay, Suffolk: Hodder and Stoughton, 1950, p. 123.

618. Cry Out with Joy. GELINEAU 99

"Cry Out with Joy to the Lord" is a nonmetrical translation of Psalm 100 which allows for the natural flow of speech. The addition of music or the process of chanting heightens the intensity of the Scripture.

The very music of the words renders them more penetrating, carries them into the heart. Because it has to overcome the noise of the world in order to be heard, the word is able to cut through indeterminate sounds by reason of its definite pitch. In borrowing from the art of sound, it sets itself apart from ordinary conversation and surpasses simple speech. He who recites Scripture without "chanting" it, says Mishnah, is an idolator. Why so, unless it is because he is dragging it down to the level of merely human speech? He profanes it by stripping it of its musical adornment, a symbol of respect by which the believer knows that it is the word of God.

(Joseph Gelineau S. J. *Voices and Instruments in Christian Worship*. London: Burns and Oates, 1964.) p. 25

Joseph Gelineau (b. 1920), a French priest, who is active today in encouraging fine congregational music making, developed a method of chanting Scripture during the 1950s. His ideas grew out of the techniques of translating the Psalms for the French version of the *Jerusalem Bible*. Translators wanted accuracy of meaning first of all, but they chose also to present the verse in its appropriate poetic structures—unlike the prose format of previous versions of Psalms—and to capture the exact rhythm of the Hebrew poetry. Father Gelineau arranged and composed music for twenty-four psalms published in French in 1953. The Ladies of the Grail in England used the French principles of translating directly from Hebrew and preserving Hebrew rhythms for their English translations published that same year.

An important principle of Hebrew poetry is that there is a fixed number of stresses for each line. In *MH* 618 there are always three recurring stresses for each line (plus an introductory stress.) Unlike metrical psalms, with their regular number of syllables per line (such as 8.6.8.6 or 8.8.8.8.), each line in a Gelineau psalm has a different number of syllables. The stresses are fixed but the number of syllables fluctuates. The words thus move freely, with the flow of natural speech.

Such a procedure is almost instinctive in the English language. Dom A. Gregory Murray explains on a recording, *The Techniques of Singing the Gelineau Psalms* (EL-20), that folk songs, nursery rhymes, and early English verse often fall into fixed stress patterns with varied numbers of syllables for lines. He uses "Three Blind Mice" to illustrate. The first line gives three slow pulses. Succeeding lines adjust their syllables to those three stresses:

(Introductory)			
	Three	blind	mice
	See	how they	run
They	all ran	af - ter the	farm - er's wife
She	cut off their	tails with the	carv - ing knife
Did you	e - ver	see such a	sight in your life
As	three	blind	mice?

The easy natural flow of this nursery rhyme should suggest the style for "Cry Out with Joy to the Lord." It will flow freely if there is only one beat for each stress—no subdivisions—and if the accents of speech are followed. Three measures of stanza 1 have three syllables each, "joy to the," "Lord all the," and "sing-ing for." The first two could be a loose ♩♪♪; "singing for" would better approximate ♪♪♪ .

The congregational antiphons, or frames for the verses, carry on the basic beat. If one chooses the third, by Dom Murray, the stress pulse (○) of the psalm verse would equal one quarter-note beat (♩=○). For antiphons 1 and 2 ♩. = ○ .

284. As the Hart with Eager Yearning.
GENEVA 42.

Descendants of European Mennonites have inherited hymns from three sixteenth-century Continental movements—Anabaptist, Lutheran, and Calvinist. The predominance of any one of these traditions in the worship of a given group in America depended on where the group had lived in Europe, when they left, where they settled in the New World, how long they retained the European language, and how much they accommodated to their surroundings. *The Mennonite Hymnal* represents a conscious attempt to restore all three traditions to Mennonite use, though the numbers of hymns and tunes in each category differs radically. There are three Anabaptist texts, nineteen sixteenth-century German texts and twenty-one tunes of the same period, and nine tunes from the Calvinist movement. (Essays on Anabaptists and Lutherans appear later in the book. This essay is concerned with the French psalters.)

John Calvin (1509-64) broke with the Roman Catholic Church in the 1530s. He was convinced that worship should be simple. Songs should be based only on texts which God had given in the Scriptures. Therefore, from 1538 to 1541, during his exile in Strasbourg, he began creating metrical versions of the psalms. He happened onto several psalms of fine quality by Clement Marot (1497-1544), valet for Francis I, King of France. Calvin included a few of these in his *Strasbourg Psalter,* 1539. By 1543 Marot had translated fifty psalms from Latin into French. Beginning in 1548 Theodore Beza (1519-1605) carried on Marot's work, publishing groups of translations until all 150 Psalms were completed in 1562. They were published, along with the Ten Commandments and Simeon's Song, in Geneva, Calvin's base of operation.

Although Calvin held austere views of the arts in worship—he considered part singing distracting and instruments unacceptable, for example—he recognized the value of good melodies. Marot had sung psalms to popular tunes in the court. Calvin found a musician, Louis Bourgeois (see p. 28), of sufficient skill and imagination to search further for existing melodies and write some of his own. The result was a collection of approximately 125 tunes for the 1562 edition; a number of them were used two or three times. They represented 110 different meters, in contrast to the English Psalter's 42.

Ambrosius Lobwasser (1515-85), a German Lutheran, began early to translate the Marot and Beza texts. He had completed a German version by 1562. Published in 1573 it has enjoyed a long history of use. The first American edition was published in Germantown, Pennsylvania, in 1753.

Mennonites in America were familiar with the Lobwasser Psalms and Genevan tunes. The first two German hymnals compiled in the United States included a number of psalms. But by the twentieth century this tradition was almost lost, as the following chart shows:

Group Publishing	Name of Book	Year	Number of Hymns	Lobwasser Psalms	Genevan tunes
Franconia Conference	*Die kleine Harfe der Kinder Zions*	1803	474	30	22
Lancaster Conference	*Ein Unpartheyisches Gesangbuch*	1804	390	62	50
Mennonite Church	*The Church Hymnal*	1927	657	0	1
General Conf. Mennonite Church	*The Mennonite Hymnary*	1940	618	0	4

The Mennonite Hymnal has revived a number of these tunes, though not necessarily those used in Pennsylvania in the early 1800s. The complete list of Genevan psalm tunes in *The Mennonite Hymnal* follows:

Genevan Psalm 1562	MH No.	Meter	Die kleine 1803	Unpart. Gesang. 1804	Church Hym. 1927	Menn. Hym. 1940
3	595	*9.8.9.8.D.*				X
12	295	*11.10.11.10.*		X		
42	284	*8.7.8.7.7.7.8.8.*	X	X		
	121					
118	607	*9.8.9.8.D.*		X		X
124	23	*10.10.10.10.10.*				
(OLD)	[447]	₍*11.10.11.10.10.*₎				[X]
134	2	*8.8.8.8.*	X	X	X	X
(OLD)	3					
136	70	*7.7.7.7.*		X		
TEN COMMAND.	407	*9.8.9.8.*				
	488					
	[264]					
SIMEON'S SONG	489	*6.6.7.D.*				

(Brackets indicate an altered version of the tune.)

This table reveals the variety of meters these tunes possess. In addition each one has an interesting arrangement of long and short notes that defies the use of one single time signature. Therefore, no signature is used in *The Mennonite Hymnal*. However, a steady beat (♩) moves through each melody. Unfortunately, the rhythmic variety and subtlety makes these tunes difficult for congregational singing. The Franconia book of 1803 retained some, though not all, of the rhythmic complexity of the originals. The Lancaster *Unpartheyisches* . . . of 1804 reduced all notes to a uniform length. The rhythm of the first phrase of GENEVA 42, for example, appears as: ♩♩♩♩♩♩♩. This might be a good way for a group to learn the notes and parts of Genevan tunes, but a congregation should have the pleasure at some point of singing the original rhythm: ♩♩♩♩♩♩♩.

The compilers of *The Mennonite Hymnal* were eager to restore the original rhythm accurately. Thus all these tunes have a half rest at the end of each phrase. That is indeed accurate, as far as we can tell in examining the sources, but it makes an awkward gap in the actual performance. It would have been better to replace the last note and rest (♩𝄽) with a whole note (𝅝) so that these tunes would correspond in editorial practice to the rest of *The Mennonite Hymnal* tunes. Although the congregation must breathe at the ends of phrases, hymnal notation does not indicate those places with rests. Future printings of *The Mennonite Hymnal* will make this editorial change.

"As the Hart with Eager Yearning" was constructed to fit the Genevan tune. An American woman, Christine Curtis (b. 1891), wrote this 1939 version of Psalm 42, which was published for the first time in *The Hymnal* of the Evangelical and Reformed Church, 1941. The last two lines of the first stanza read originally·

When shall I abide rejoicing
In His presence, His praise voicing.

The alteration is extensive enough to warrant a ‡ sign after the translator's name. Christine Curtis published several books of poetry, the most recent in 1961.

Louis Bourgeois was responsible for the composing or arranging of GENEVA 42. The Germans borrowed it as a common tune for a number of texts, though its first German text, "Freu dich sehr, o meine Seele," appeared in 1620. Thus it is often labeled FREU DICH SEHR in hymnals. Bach used it in his cantatas with five different texts, one of which— "Tröstet, tröstet"—stands in English at *MH* 121.

30. Angels Holy, High, and Lowly.
WINDMERE

The Psalms formed the collection of songs for the Children of Israel, but there are additional songs, known as *canticles,* throughout the Old and New Testaments. The Book of Luke yields several canticles. The most famous is Mary's song, the *Magnificat,* which is sung at Vespers in the Roman Catholic Church and in Anglican Evensong. Simeon's song, the *Nunc Dimittis,* is sung at sundown in Compline—also in Evensong. The song of Zacharias is used in Lauds, at dawn.

The *Benedicite,* on which "Angels Holy" *MH* 30 is based, is a part of Lauds on Feast Days, but it comes from the Old Testament—the Book of Daniel in the Greek, or *Septuagint,* version. Because it is not in the Hebrew version of Daniel we have to look for it among the apocryphal writings and insert it in chapter 3 between verses 23 and 24. The *Apocrypha* includes the *Benedicite* in the chapter "The Prayer of Azariah and the Song of the Three Young Men."

Here is the translation of the "Song of the Three Young Men" from the Anglican *Book of Common Prayer,* where it appears with Morning Prayer: (Notice that the men in the fiery furnace praise God for fire!)

O all ye Works of the Lord, bless ye the Lord: praise him, and magnify him for ever.

O ye Angels of the Lord, bless ye the Lord: praise him, and magnify him for ever.

O ye Heavens, bless ye the Lord: praise him, and magnify him for ever.

O ye Waters that be above the firmament, bless ye the Lord: praise him, and magnify him for ever.

O all ye Powers of the Lord, bless ye the Lord: praise him, and magnify him for ever.

O ye Sun and Moon, bless ye the Lord: praise him, and magnify him for ever.

O ye Stars of heaven, bless ye the Lord: praise him, and magnify him for ever.

O ye Showers and Dew, bless ye the Lord: praise him, and magnify him for ever.

O ye Winds of God, bless ye the Lord: praise him, and magnify him for ever.

O ye Fire and Heat, bless ye the Lord: praise him, and magnify him for ever.

O ye Winter and Summer, bless ye the Lord: praise him, and magnify him for ever.

O ye Dews and Frosts, bless ye the Lord: praise him, and magnify him for ever.

O ye Ice and Snow, bless ye the Lord: praise him, and magnify him for ever.

O ye Nights and Days, bless ye the Lord: praise him, and magnify him for ever.

O ye Light and Darkness, bless ye the Lord: praise him, and magnify him for ever.

O ye Lightnings and Clouds, bless ye the Lord: praise him, and magnify him for ever.

O let the Earth bless the Lord: yea, let it praise him, and magnify him for ever.

O ye Mountains and Hills bless ye the Lord: praise him, and magnify him for ever.

O all ye Green Things upon the earth, bless ye the Lord: praise him, and magnify him for ever.

O ye Wells, bless ye the Lord: praise him, and magnify him for ever.

O ye Seas and Floods, bless ye the Lord: praise him, and magnify him for ever.

O ye Whales, and all that move in the waters, bless the Lord: praise him, and magnify him for ever.

O all ye Fowls of the air, bless ye the Lord: praise him, and magnify him for ever.

O all ye Beasts and Cattle bless ye the Lord: praise him, and magnify him for ever.

O ye Children of Men, bless ye the Lord: praise him, and magnify him for ever.

O let Israel bless the Lord: praise him, and magnify him for ever.

O ye Priests of the Lord, bless ye the Lord: praise him, and magnify him for ever.

O ye Servants of the Lord, bless ye the Lord: praise him, and magnify him for ever.

O ye Spirits and Souls of the Righteous, bless ye the Lord: praise him, and magnify him for ever.

O ye holy and humble Men of heart, bless ye the Lord: praise him, and magnify him for ever.

For centuries and until 1964, when the Roman Catholic Church changed to the vernacular languages, they sang the *Benedicite* framed by an antiphon which fit the particular season. At Christmas, for example, the antiphon said, "There was with the angel a multitude of the heavenly host, praising and saying, 'Glory to God in the highest and on earth peace to men of good will; alleluia!' "

John Stuart Blackie (1809-95) was a Scottish scholar of classical Greek and Latin. Julian's *Dictionary of Hymnology* quotes Blackie's comment that he wrote "Angels Holy" "for a beautiful Burschen melody, *Alles Schweige*" and published it first in *Tait's Magazine* in 1840. It was included in Bonar's *Bible Hymn Book,* 1845, and again in Blackie's own *Legends of Ancient Greece, with other Poems,* 1857. The latter version, printed in *Lyra Britannica,* 1867, supplies the stanzas missing from *MH* 30, which uses only stanzas 1, 6, and 7.

2.   Sun and moon bright,
          Night and moonlight,
    Starry temples azure-floor'd,

Cloud and rain, and wild winds' madness,
Sons of God that shout for gladness,
Praise ye, praise ye, God the Lord!

3.   Ocean hoary,
             Tell His glory,
Cliffs, where tumbling seas have roar'd!
Pulse of waters, blithely beating,
Wave advancing, wave retreating,
Praise ye, praise ye, God the Lord!

4.   Rock and high land,
             Wood and island,
Crag, where eagle's pride hath soar'd,
Mighty mountains, purple-breasted,
Peaks cloud-cleaving, snowy-crested,
Praise ye, praise ye, God the Lord!

5.   Rolling river,
             Praise Him ever,
From the mountain's deep vein pour'd,
Silver fountain, clearly gushing,
Troubled torrent, madly rushing,
Praise ye, praise ye, God the Lord!

Charles Frederick Maker (1844-1927), who wrote the tune, WINDER-MERE, was a Bristol organist, who contributed a number of tunes to the *Bristol Tune Book,* 1863. WINDERMERE is No. 717 in the third series edition, 1891. (Other Maker tunes are *MH* 171, 225, 267, 409, 512.)

MH 30 presents the tune and parts exactly as they appear in the original (with notes halved in *The Mennonite Hymnal*) except for the dynamics indicated. Although dynamics are rarely shown in the *Bristol Tune Book,* WINDERMERE begins *p,* introduces a *crescendo* at "Sing the praises," arriving at *f* at "Earth and sky." The refrain, "Praise ye" is *ff.* The wide range of dynamics was a part of the fashion of the times. But even though Tchaikowsky has a range of *pppppp* to *fffff* in some of his orchestral works, *p* to *f* in a hymn represents a very rapid change over so short a period of time. Present performance practice tends to maintain a more even, uniform level of loud or soft. Nevertheless, Maker's music depends a good deal more on manipulated dynamics than does that of Louis Bourgeois or Joseph Gelineau. The sequential repetition of:

in the last half of WINDERMERE, for example, naturally swells to the highest note and creates enough momentum for a loud conclusion.

1. Holy God, We Praise Thy Name.
GROSSER GOTT WIR LOBEN DICH.

The *Te Deum laudamus* is a canticle much more familiar than the *Benedicite*. Julian called it "the most famous nonbiblical hymn of the Western world" (p. 1119). Its source is unknown, but the legend persists that Saints Ambrose and Augustine improvised it at Augustine's baptism in A.D. 385. It is ascribed to them as recently as 1895 in the *Liber Responsorialis*.[1]

Hymnus SS. Ambrosii et Augustini.

I. Tonus Solemnis.

Figure 8

Liber Responsorialis [*pro Festis I. Classis et Communi Sanctorum. Juxta Ritum Monasticum.*]
Solesmis: E Typographeo Sancti Petri, 1895.

The Latin prose was translated into an English prose version which is still in use for Morning Prayer in Anglican worship, although the

Benedictus of Zacharias or the *Benedicite,* "The Song of the Three Young Men," can be substituted.

In the *Book of Common Prayer* it is set up in three clear sections of 7, 8, and 7 sentences.[2] The first section is a song of praise, the second, a confession of faith, and the third, a prayer for help.

1a We praise thee, O God; we acknowledge thee to be the Lord.
All the earth doth worship thee, the Father everlasting.
To thee all angels cry aloud; the Heavens, and all the Powers therein;
To thec Cherubim and Seraphim continually do cry,
Holy, Holy, Holy, Lord God of Sabaoth;
Heaven and earth are full of the Majesty of thy glory.

1b The glorious company of Apostles praise thee.
The goodly fellowship of the prophets praise thee.
The noble army of Martyrs praise thee.
The holy Church throughout all the world doth acknowledge thee;
The Father, of an infinite Majesty;
Thine adorable, true, and only Son;
Also the Holy Ghost, the Comforter.

2 Thou art the King of Glory, O Christ.
Thou art the everlasting Son of the Father.
When thou tookest upon thee to deliver man, thou didst humble thyself to be born of a Virgin.
When thou hast overcome the sharpness of death, thou didst open the Kingdom of Heaven to all believers.
Thou sittest at the right hand of God, in the glory of the Father.
We believe that thou shalt come to be our Judge.
We therefore pray thee, help thy servants, whom thou hast redeemed with thy precious blood.
Make them to be numbered with thy Saints, in glory everlasting.

3 O Lord, save thy people, and bless thine heritage.
Govern them, and lift them up for ever.
Day by day we magnify thee;
And worship thy Name ever, world without end.
Vouchsafe, O Lord, to keep us this day without sin.
O Lord, have mercy upon us, have mercy upon us.
O Lord, let thy mercy be upon us, as our trust is in thee.
O Lord, in thee have I trusted; let me never be confounded.

Because the text is frequently used, many English composers from the late sixteenth century to the present day, have made musical settings.

MH 1 consists of a cento (a portion of the whole poem) by Clarence Walworth (1820-1900). An American who became a Roman Catholic in 1845, Walworth helped to found the order of Paulist Fathers. The cento is the first of the three parts. The first six lines (1a)—three sentences—end with the exclamation, "Holy, Holy, Holy." The next seven lines (1b)—four sentences—draw in the apostles, prophets, martyrs, and the whole Church to sing a Trinitarian doxology.

Walworth's three stanzas omitted in *MH* 1 paraphrase the remainder of the *Te Deum:*

5 Thou art King of Glory, Christ!
   Son of God, yet born of Mary.
   For us sinners sacrificed,
     And to death a Tributary,
   First to break the bars of death,
   Thou hast opened Heaven to faith.

6 From Thy high, celestial Home,
   Judge of all, again returning,
   We believe that Thou shalt come,
     On the dreadful Doom's-day morning,
   When Thy Voice shall shake the earth,
   And the startled dead come forth.

7 Spare Thy people, Lord, we pray,
     By a thousand snares surrounded:
   Keep us without sin today,
     Never let us be confounded.
   Lo! I put my trust in Thee,
   Never, Lord, abandon me.

Luther valued the *Te Deum* highly and placed it alongside of the Apostles' Creed and the Athanasian Creed in importance.[3] He made a rhymed version in German around 1529 and a prose translation in 1538. The Wittenberg Church order of 1533 stated: "After the hymn let the choir intone the *Te Deum laudamus,* in Dr. Martin's German translation, and let one of the choristers in the schoolboys' pew answer with the congregation in half-verses."[4] Mennonites have sung and continue to sing the *Te Deum* in German.

Ignaz Franz was probably the author of the metrical paraphrase, "Grosser Gott, wir loben dich," for Maria Theresa's book, *Katholisches Gesangbuch,* c. 1774. Franz was a Roman Catholic hymnologist who compiled several hymnbooks, including this one for the Empress of Austria. His version had twelve stanzas, of which stanzas 1, 2, 5, and 9 appear beneath the English text and the music of *MH* 1. (The Canadian

Gesangbuch Der Mennoniten, 1965, uses stanza 6 in addition.)

The composer for GROSSER GOTT is unknown. The Newberry Library in Chicago has a 1776 copy of Maria Theresa's book, in which the music is given in 6/8, a dance-like meter. The texture is often only three-part rather than four. (See Figure 9.) The tune came into Protestant use through J. G. Schicht's *Choralbuch,* 1819, and, with slight alterations, became HURSLEY, *MH* 491 (combined with "Sun of My Soul" by John Keble and named for his parish).

Figure 9

Maria Theresa's *Katholishes Gesangbuch, c.1774*
Ignaz Franz
Facsimile reprint, courtesy of the Newberry Library

Gesangbuch mit Noten, 1890, included GROSSER GOTT not only with its proper text, but also as a common tune for eleven other texts. The Canadian *Gesangbuch Der Mennoniten,* 1965, has four common-tune appearances of GROSSER GOTT.

The *Te Deum* is the basis also for *MH* 28. "O God, We Praise Thee" appeared in the *Supplement to the New Version of Psalms,* around 1700. Tate and Brady published this Psalter first in 1696 and called it the *New Version,* making Sternhold and Hopkins' Psalter of 1562 the Old Version (from which tunes are called "old," as OLD HUNDREDTH). *The Mennonite Hymnal* includes Tate and Brady Psalms at 14, 41, and 285.

The metrical version of *Te Deum* has seven stanzas of common meter double (C.M.D.), with a proper tune and bass. Here is the melody, from the 1708 Supplement:

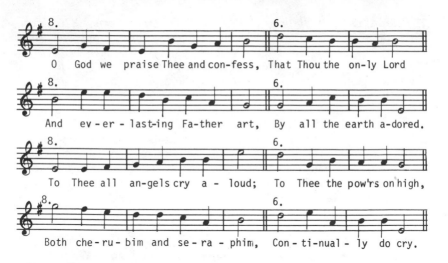

O God we praise Thee and con-fess, That Thou the on-ly Lord

And ev-er-last-ing Fa-ther art, By all the earth a-dored.

To Thee all an-gels cry a-loud; To Thee the pow'rs on high,

Both che-ru-bim and se-ra-phim, Con-ti-nual-ly do cry.

For *MH* 28 we have an older common meter (C.M.) tune instead, TALLIS' ORDINAL, 8.6.8.6. only; therefore each long original stanza makes two short stanzas. It is one of the very earliest tunes in common meter, coming from the 1560s. (See p. 59 for Tallis.) Because it was written for *Veni Creator*[5] for use at ordinations of bishops and priests and appeared in the Anglican book called *The Ordinal,* it has retained the name, TALLIS' ORDINAL.

[1] It is difficult to prove or disprove this attribution. In 1894, however, Dom G. Morin pointed to evidences that Niceta of Remesiana, a missionary bishop of the fourth century, wrote the *Te Deum.* In 1926, A. E. Burns wrote an entire book of 86 pages supporting this view (*The Hymn Te Deum and Its Author.* London: Faith Press).

[2] Burns, in examining the Latin text, finds "3 stanzas of 4 lines, each line beginning with 'Thou,' 'Thee,' or 'To Thee,' while each stanza was followed by a refrain in shorter lines, introduced by a key word, v. 4, 'do cry,' v. 10, 'acknowledge,' v. 20, 'pray.' " (p. 6) The *Te Deum* closes with prayers.

[3] *Luther's Works,* vol. 53, *Liturgy and Hymns,* ed. by U. S. Leupold, p. 171.

[4] *Ibid.,* 173.

[5] *Veni Creator Spiritus,* text at *MH* 211.

292. The Sands of Time Are Sinking.
RUTHERFORD.

Annie Ross Cousin's poem "Immanuel's Land," with the subtitle "The Last Words of Samuel Rutherford," appeared first in *Christian Treasury,*

1857, and again in *Immanuel's Land and Other Poems,* 1876. Annie Cousin (1824-1906), the wife of a Scottish Free Church minister, wove together fragments from letters and dying sayings of Samuel Rutherford. McCutcheon identifies Rutherford as "the persecuted Scottish divine of the seventeenth century" (*Hymn Tune Names,* p. 123). His parish at Anwoth figures in the poem several times.

Few present-day hymnals include the hymn. Almost one hundred years ago Julian said of Cousin's poems that "many are very beautiful. In general they are, however, rather meditations than suited to public worship." The handbook writers of the few churches that still sing "The Sands of Time" repeat that rather faint praise. Yet I know a number of persons who find this hymn unusually compelling, and it stands at the top of my own childhood memories of worship. In spite of my mistaking the sand of the hourglass for sinking quicksand, I loved the song, which still holds a kind of magic for me.

The many poetic images catch one's imagination. Most of our hymns are full of abstractions. Images make us vaguely uneasy. What do they mean? The *Church Hymnal,* 1927, had quotation marks around "house of wine" in stanza 5 of "The Sands of Time"—undoubtedly to control the image and make it perfectly clear.

Incidentally, *The Mennonite Hymnal's* earliest hymn in the English language, number 645, is built on the concrete and abstract, presented in pairs:

God be in my head, and in my understanding;
God be in mine eyes, and in my looking;
God be in my mouth, and in my speaking;
God be in my heart, and in my thinking.

When this hymn first came to my congregation in the 1950s, a few people were troubled by the concrete member of the pair. Head, eyes, and mouth seemed too direct; understanding, looking, speaking, and thinking had the necessary psychological distance.

At any rate, I am grateful for hymns like, *MH* 292 and 645 and others like "Come O Thou Traveller Unknown" and "O Have You Not Heard of That Beautiful Stream?", whose images are strong. I wish for more of them to speak to the imaginations of the children in our congregations.

"The Sands of Time" had 19 stanzas. *MH* 292 includes 1, 5, 11, 13, 15, and 17. The remaining stanzas follow from the 1876 edition of the author's poems:

2 Oh! well it is for ever,
   Oh! well for evermore,
  My nest hung in no forest
   Of all this death-doomed shore;

Yea, let the vain world vanish,
  As from the ship the strand,
Since glory—glory dwelleth
  In Immanuel's Land.

44

3 There the red Rose of Sharon
   Unfolds its heartmost bloom,
And fills the air of Heaven
   With ravishing perfume:
Oh! to behold it blossom,
   While by its fragrance fanned,
Where glory—glory dwelleth
   In Immanuel's Land.

4 The King there, in His beauty,
   Without a veil is seen:
It were a well-spent journey,
   Though seven deaths lay between:
The Lamb with His fair army,
   Doth on Mount Zion stand,
And glory—glory dwelleth
   In Immanuel's Land.

6 E'en Anwoth was not heaven
   E'en preaching was not Christ;
And in my sea-beat prison
   My Lord and I held tryst:
And aye my murkiest storm-cloud
   Was by a rainbow spanned,
Caught from the glory dwelling
   In Immanuel's Land.

7 But that He built a Heaven
   Of His surpassing love,
A little New Jerusalem,
   Like to the one above,
"Lord, take me o'er the water,"
   Had been my loud demand,
"Take me to love's own country,
   Unto Immanuel's Land."

8 But flowers need night's cool darkness,
   The moonlight and the dew;
So Christ, from one who loved it,
   His shining oft withdrew:
And then, for cause of absence,
   My troubled soul I scanned;
But glory, shadeless, dwelleth
   In Immanuel's Land.

9 The little birds of Anwoth
   I used to count them blest,
Now, beside happier altars
   I go to build my nest:
O'er these there broods no silence,
   No graves around them stand,
For glory, deathless, dwelleth
   In Immanuel's Land.

10 Fair Anwoth by the Solway,
   To me thou still art dear!
E'en on the verge of Heaven
   I drop for thee a tear.
Oh! if one soul from Anwoth
   Meet me at God's right hand,
My Heaven will be two Heavens
   In Immanuel's Land.

12 Deep waters crossed life's pathway,
   The hedge of thorns was sharp:
Now, these lie all behind me,—
   Oh for a well-tuned harp!
Oh! to join Halleluiah
   With yon triumphant band,
Who sing, where glory dwelleth,
   In Immanuel's Land.

14 Soon shall the cup of glory
   Wash down earth's bitterest woes,
Soon shall the desert briar
   Break into Eden's rose;
The curse shall change to blessing,
   The name on earth that's banned,
Be graven on the white stone
   In Immanuel's Land.

16 I shall sleep sound in Jesus,
   Filled with His likeness rise,
To live and to adore Him,
   To see Him with these eyes:
'Tween me and resurrection,
   But Paradise doth stand;
Then—then for glory dwelling
   In Immanuel's Land.

18 I have borne scorn and hatred,
   I have borne wrong and shame,
Earth's proud ones have reproached me,
   For Christ's thrice blessed name:
Where God His seal set fairest,
   They've stamped their foulest brand;
But judgment shines like noonday
   In Immanuel's Land.

19 They've summoned me before them,
   But there I may not come,—
My Lord says, "Come up hither,"
   My Lord says, "Welcome Home!"
My kingly King, at His white throne.
   My presence doth command,
Where glory—glory dwelleth
   In Immanuel's Land.

RUTHERFORD, named, of course, for the Samuel Rutherford of the text, was arranged by Edward Francis Rimbault (1816-76) from a French tune, by C. Urban (1790-1845), published in *Chants Chretiéns* in Paris in 1834. The tune should by all logical analyses be dreary, but that has not been my experience. The music has somehow seemed to fit our four-part unaccompanied singing remarkably well, and has made an excellent vehicle for the text for a particular group of people at a particular time and place.

I suspect that the particular, local qualities of hymn singing have much to do with our judgment of what is good. Like the masks in *Arrow of God,* by the Nigerian novelist, Chinua Achebe, hymns are functional and communal. After a group of persons had commissioned the mask in appropriate secrecy, Edogo the mask-carver followed carefully the traditional procedures for constructing it. He worried a bit about its quality, but he waited until its ritual appearance at the festival to judge its worth. "Edogo knew . . . that he must see the Mask in action to know whether it was good or bad."[1]

Hymns, too, must be judged in action. They are meant to function in a group—to serve as vehicles for expression and communication of praise, to trigger associations beyond the usual linear time frame, to touch individual and group memories and aspirations, to stimulate imagination, and to draw believers together in a unified focus on God and his action among them.

[1] London: Heinemann, 1964, p. 251.

524-525. Praise to God, Immortal Praise. PRAYER and ORIENTIS PARTIBUS.

Anna Laetitia Barbauld (1743-1825), the English author of "Praise to God, Immortal Praise," was the daughter of a Dissenting minister of French Protestant background and was married to a Dissenting minister.

This text first appeared in a book by William Enfield, *Hymns for Public Worship,* 1772, with the subtitle, "Praise to God in Prosperity and Adversity." When it was printed the next year in Anna Barbauld's *Poems,* the reference to Habakkuk 3:17, 18 (KJV) accompanied the text:

Although the fig tree shall not blossom, neither shall fruit be in the vines; the labor of the olive shall fail, and the fields shall yield no meat;

47

the flock shall be cut off from the fold, and there shall be no herd in the stalls:
Yet I will rejoice in the Lord, I will joy in the God of my salvation.

The Index of Scriptural Allusions in *The Mennonite Hymnal* lists *MH* 253 in addition to *MH* 525 for the Habakkuk passage. It is worthwhile to see these poems side by side.

"Praise to God" enjoyed a wide use, especially in the nineteenth century. It usually appeared as a cento—normally the first four or five stanzas—and was revised rather extensively. *Hymns and Tunes,* 1890, included the five stanzas and revisions of *MH* 524. The last half of stanza 2 originally read: "For the vine's exalted juice, For the generous olive's use." Stanza 3 said: "Clouds that drop their fattening dews." (Incidentally, one Mennonite meteorologist recently wrote to urge correcting the concept that clouds drop dew.) The stanza went on: "Suns that temperate warmth diffuse." These two phrases formed the last half of stanza 3. As is usual with alterations, the lines substituted are far more general than the original. A few additional word changes were made.

The *Mennonite Hymnal, a Blending of Many Voices,* 1894, also had five stanzas. These remained close to the Barbauld original, changing only in the last half of stanza 2: "For the fruits in full supply, Ripened 'neath the summer sky." The text was not carried on in the General Conference Mennonite books of 1927 and 1940.

The compilers of *The Mennonite Hymnal* decided to honor the "prosperity and adversity" intention of the original poem. They changed the first word of stanza 6 from *yet* to *Lord* and made a second hymn—the one for times of crop failure, or other forms of adversity. But a congregation could choose a few stanzas from each half and use one tune throughout. They could choose another tune, for that matter. Other American hymnals which include "Praise to God" combine it with DIX, the tune we use with "For the Beauty of the Earth."

The *Church and Sunday Hymnal,* 1902, introduced the tune, PRAYER, to the Mennonite Church, and the 1927 *Church Hymnal* continued its use. The earliest appearance of the tune that I have found is *The Devotional Harmonist: A Collection of Sacred Music,* published for a group of Methodist Episcopal Churches near New York, in 1850. The book, in an oblong format, consists of an introduction to the elements of vocal music and 385 pages of music. The musical editor, Charles Dingley, described the music of the collection thus:

> While the music generally is flowing and melodious in its character, it is of a style perfectly simple and intelligible, so as to be easily sung. All points of imitation and needless difficulties in the construction of the harmony have been avoided. "Simple and natural harmony,"—rich without being abstruse, pleasing without being paltry—"is vastly better adapted to impress the heart, and promote devotional feeling,

than the most highly wrought pieces of chromatic skill" (Editor's Preface).

PRAYER appears at page 227 in Dingley with the text, "Gracious Spirit—Love Divine," in the key of D, with the melody in the tenor. There is so little activity in the soprano and bass parts that the music may seem "paltry"—certainly not "abstruse"—to persons first encountering it. It works best for unaccompanied, four-part singing, which probably explains why, to my knowledge, no other hymnals presently include it. Asahel Abbot is given as the composer. His works are present in American books of the 1840s and 1850s, but details of his life are not known.

ORIENTIS PARTIBUS is a thirteenth-century, folk-like, sacred song. Although authorities differ on some of the details, they agree that it was a melody written by Pierre de Corbeil (d. 1222), Archbishop of Sens, for use in his cathedral. Its text, the famous "Song of the Ass," was probably used in the Office of the Feast of Circumcision, January 1. The ass was remembered for carrying the Holy Family to Egypt and bringing the Magi from the East (which seems to be the intent here). The song is a conductus,[1] an escorting or processional piece, and it is very similar in style to the secular songs of the troubadours of the period. Songs of its type were included in liturgical drama.

Stanza 1 has a clear meter (7.7.7.7.5.) and a repetitious rhyme scheme; both the meter and rhyme patterns carry on throughout the nine stanzas.

1 Orientis partibus
   Adventavit asinus,
   Pulcher et fortissimus,
   Sarcinis aptissimus.
   Hez, sir asne, hez! (refrain)

Translation:
   Out from lands of Orient
   Was the ass divinely sent;
   Strong and very fair was he,
   Bearing burdens gallantly.
   Heigh, Sir Ass, oh heigh!

Three additional stanzas in English:
3 Higher leap'd than goats can bound,
   Doe and roebuck circled round;
   Median dromedaries speed
   Overcame, and took the lead.
   Heigh, Sir Ass, oh heigh!

4 While he drags long carriages,

Loaded down with baggages,
He, with jaws insatiate,
Fodder hard doth masticate.
Heigh, Sir Ass, oh heigh!

6 Stuff'd with grass, yet speak and say
Amen, Ass, with every bray;
Amen, Amen, say again,
Ancient sins hold in disdain.
Heigh, Sir Ass, oh heigh![2]

Notation of the thirteenth century did not clarify the question of musical meter, that is, its organization in 2s or 3s. Therefore one finds either meter in modern transcriptions; 3s would appear: ♩♩|♩♩♩|♩♩♩|♩.|. *MH* 525 has duple time, as arranged by Richard Redhead (1820-1901), one of the leaders in reviving Gregorian chant.

This is probably the earliest example in *The Mennonite Hymnal* of a secular musical style transformed into church music.

[1] See Jacques Handschin, "Trope, Sequence, and Conductus," in the *New Oxford History of Music.* London: Oxford University Press, 1954. Pages 171-74.
[2] Translated by H. C. Green, *Speculum,* vol. VI, 1931, p. 535.

487. The Duteous Day Now Closeth.
O WELT, ICH MUSS DICH LASSEN.
(INNSBRUCK).

Ever since Luther developed a new type of vernacular hymnody in his Reformation movement, Anabaptists and Mennonites have been borrowing Lutheran hymns, known as *chorales.* The *Mennonite Hymnary,* 1940, had sixty-five chorale texts and tunes, because many General Conference Mennonites had emigrated recently from Europe. The Mennonite Church's *Church Hymnal,* 1927, had only three hymns that were clearly chorales; a few other hymns had chorale texts, but the tunes were altered radically in the direction of English meters. However, a number of generations earlier, the chorale had been familiar material for the (Old) Mennonites in America also. Although *Die kleine Harfe* and *Unpartheyisches Gesangbuch* of 1803 and 1804 (see p. 34) opened with Calvinist psalms, the large bulk of their contents were chorales.

The Mennonite Hymnal, 1969, has ninety-two German texts, including three Anabaptist hymns and several hymns written for German Roman

Catholics. Forty-nine of the texts are paired with their "proper tunes." This means that the German tune name is the same as the German text identification on the top left of the hymn. Another twenty-one chorale tunes are matched with German texts, though not in the original combination. Therefore, the tune name differs from the German text identification, as is the case with "The Duteous Day." There are two tune names: O WELT, ICH MUSS DICH LASSEN and INNSBRUCK ICH MUSS DICH LASSEN, neither of which matches the poem, *Nun ruhen alle Wälder.* The melody thus functions as a common tune for a chorale text.

The earliest chorales were Luther's "A Mighty Fortress," *MH* 325 and 597, and excerpts from the German Mass, such as "O Lamb of God All Holy," *MH* 173. Two great chorales by Philipp Nicolai—"Wake, Awake for Night Is Flying," *MH* 118, and "How Bright Appears the Morning Star," *MH* 141 were written at the close of the sixteenth century. In the seventeenth century the conflicts of the Thirty Years' War (1618-48) changed the character of what people wanted to sing. Paul Gerhardt (1607-76), who wrote eight of the texts in *The Mennonite Hymnal,* moved away from the vigorous, objective character of his predecessors' hymns toward a more personal and intimate expression. Three of those in *The Mennonite Hymnal*—17, 119, and 124—have a cheerful quality. Although the remaining five poems—159, 266, 338, 340, and 487—express strong faith and confidence in God's love, their ethos is dominated by words like "sorrow," "anguish," "abuse," "fear," "care," and "suffering." Gerhardt could have found reason for despair in his private losses—his wife, four of his five children, and his job in Berlin—but the poems of some of his contemporaries are so similar in mood that he seems to have captured skillfully the character of the times. (See also Heermann, *MH* 158 and 352; Neumark, 314; Rinckart, 31.)

Robert Bridges (1844-1930) made the translation for *Nun ruhen alle Wälder.* All of his translations or paraphrases in *The Mennonite Hymnal* were a part of the remarkable *Yattendon Hymnal,* whose texts he edited in 1899. H. Ellis Wooldridge (1845-1917) edited the tunes and contributed a few of his own (*MH* 603). Bridges made English versions of Latin poems, *MH* 211 and 604, Greek, *MH* 489, and German *MH* 158, 291, and 487.

The editors Bridges and Wooldridge set very high standards for the 100 hymns of their book. The Synopsis of the Music in Order of Date begins with Plainsong, or Chant melodies, then includes eight composers of the sixteenth century, seven of the seventeenth, three from the eighteenth, and only Wooldridge from the nineteenth. The prolific, nineteenth-century tune writers were conspicuously absent.

The *Yattendon Hymnal* must surely be the most elegant hymnbook ever published. It is quarto size, printed on fine, heavy paper. The unusual type was based on a type design by an Oxford printer of the

1680s, Peter de Walpergen. (The *Oxford Hymn Book,* 1908, also used Walpergen type. See p. 22.) There are two shapes for heads and notes, and the stems are placed carefully for the finest artistic effect. Figure 10 shows the first phrase of INNSBRUCK from the 1905 edition.

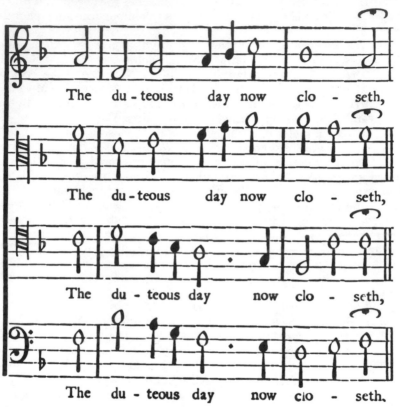

Figure 10

Hymns/The Yattendon Hymnal
Oxford: B. H. Blackwell, 1905, No. 83.

Bridges wrote essays on various aspects of hymnody. In his essay, "Practical Discourse on some Principles of Hymn-Singing," 1899, he made a footnote comment on the lack of quality in texts. (The spelling here is Bridges's; he worked on several alternatives to English spelling.)

When one turns the pages of thatt most depressing of all books ever compiled by the groaning creatur, Julian's hymn-dictionary, and sees the thousands of carefully tabulated English hymns, by far the greater number of them not only pitiable as efforts of human intelligence, but absolutely worthless as vocal material and melodic treatment, one wishes that all this effort had been directed to supply a real want. E.g. the two Wesleys between them wrote thirteen octavo volumes, of some 400 pages each, full of closely printed hymns. One must wish that Charles Wesley at least (who show'd in a few instances how well he could do) had, instead of reeling off all this stuff, concentrated his efforts to produce only what should be worthy of his talents and useful to posterity. [1]

And in a private letter to Lady Mary Trefusis, 1911, Bridges said some startling things about the relationship between text and music—surprising in light of his stature as a poet.

I could only approach the subject of words from the musical point of view—and then one of the proper questions that would first arise would be the relation of words to music; and here, how far the artistic form of the hymn-tunes renders the tunes independent of the grammar of the words; e.g. whether the accented notes in the tune require always a corresponding accent in the words. I think that the intelligent hymn-singer is getting much too squeamish on this head. I do not find that an occasional disagreement between accent of words and music offends me in a hymn. A fine tune is an unalterable artistic form, which pleases in itself and for itself. The notion of its giving way to the words is impossible. The words are better suited if they fit in with *all* the quantities and accents of the tune, but it is almost impossible and not necessary that they should. Their *mood* is what the tune must be true to; and the mood is the main thing. If the tune also incidentally reinforces important words or phrases, thatt is all the better, and where ther are refrains, or repetitions of words the tune should be design'd for them; but the enormous power that the tune has of enforcing or even of creating a mood is the one invaluable thing of magnitude, which overrules every other consideration. [2]

The tune for *MH* 487, O WELT, ICH MUSS DICH LASSEN ("O World, I must leave you"), is a fine example of the transformation of a secular song to sacred use. Many authorities are convinced that this tune existed first as a German folk tune before it was notated as a *Wanderlied—Innsbruck, ich muss dich lassen.* Legend attributes the text to the Emperor Maximilian of Austria and the tune to his court musician, Heinrich Isaac. Johannes Kulp in *Handbuch zum Evangelischen Kirchengesangbuch* points to 1505 as the earliest sacred use of the folk tune—in a song of St. Anna and Joachim. [3]

We do know that a four-part polyphonic version by Isaac (c. 1450-1517) appeared in Förster's *Frischen Teutscher Liedlein,* 1539. There the melody was in the upper voice. He also made a four-part instrumental setting with the melody in the tenor, imitated in canon by the alto. He used the melody further in the tenor voice of the "Christe eleison" of his *Missa Carminum,* a folk-tune Mass published in 1541.

J. S. Bach used the melody in three of his cantatas and in two passions. *The Mennonite Hymnal* version is number 16 of the *Passion According to St. Matthew.* By Bach's day the original, flexible rhythm of the melody was regularized. Both Isaac and Bach used a 7.7.6.7.7.8. poetic meter, but the rhythmic treatment differed:

Isaac:

Bach:

(transposed down a step)

We can see the trend toward regularizing by comparing also the two versions of EIN FESTE BURG in *The Mennonite Hymnal. MH* 597 has the original, vigorous rhythm; *MH* 325, a later form, is reduced to balanced measures which create a square effect. Why this change took place during the seventeenth century in chorales as well as psalm tunes is hard to determine with certainty. It might be that congregations gradually equalized notes because unequal relations are in some ways more difficult for a group to sing. Perhaps trends in dance rhythms influenced hymns toward regular 2s or 3s. Or the temper of rationalism may have subtly moved tastes toward regularity and clarity.

In any case, Bach compensated for the rhythmic dullness by creating a harmonic rhythm of great complexity. His four parts make vertical chords that move in and out of tension and resolution continually, without losing the independence of four interesting horizontal lines. Further Bach versions in *The Mennonite Hymnal* can be found at 136, 159, 352, 453, 599, 600, 609, and 611.

A further change in the tune, typical of the nineteenth-century use of the past, came with Lowell Mason's CLINTON, published in *The National Psalmist,* 1848, and identified as, "Arranged from an Old Tune by H. Isaac, 1490." He altered the poetic meter to 8.8.6.8.8.6.. Here is the first half for comparison with Isaac and Bach:

(transposed down a step)

The compilers of *The Mennonite Hymnal* returned to the early rhythmic versions of chorale tunes in many cases, recognizing that, in spite of their difficulty for congregational use, they would be rewarding. (Examples are: *MH* 60, 91, 118, 141, 178, 264, and 406.)

[1] *Collected Essays of Robert Bridges* XXI-XXVI. London: Oxford University Press, 1935, p. 52.
[2] *Ibid.*, 70-71.
[3] Göttingen: Vandenhoeck & Ruprecht, 1958, p. 485.

14. O Come, Loud Anthems Let Us Sing. SALISBURY.

Psalm singing was the normal diet of English Reformation worship. In this respect the British followed the lead of John Calvin rather than Martin Luther.

Thomas Sternhold (1500-49), the Groom of the Robes for Henry VIII, seems to have been the first person to borrow the popular ballad meter, consisting of pairs of fourteeners, or 8.6.8.6., for singing psalms. Julian says, "He hoped that the courtiers would sing them instead of their amorous and obscene songs" (p. 861i). Sternhold wrote forty metrical psalms in all. John Hopkins (d. 1570), who arranged sixty metrical psalms, along with several other poets, such as William Kethe (*MH* 2), completed the whole Book of 150 Psalms by 1562. The collection is often called *Sternhold and Hopkins,* or the *Old Version.*

During the next hundred years or so many poets tried to improve upon the Old Version. The King James Version of the Bible, 1611, and the writings of poets such as William Shakespeare, must have influenced the English language profoundly during the early seventeenth century. By 1696 Nahum Tate (1652-1715)—the same man who wrote the libretto for Purcell's *Dido and Aeneas*—and Nicholas Brady (1659-1726) had prepared a *New Version of the Psalms of David.* "O Come, Loud Anthems Let Us Sing" is Psalm 95 from the New Version, with a refrain added from Isaac Watts's *Psalms* of 1719, where it functioned as a refrain for Psalm 104.

Two important Psalters came between the Old and New Versions. The Puritans brought out the *Bay Psalm Book* in 1640, the first book to be published in North America. They were dissatisfied with the translation of the Old Version because "it was too free for their taste." [1] The Pilgrims had a version translated directly from the Hebrew by Henry Ainsworth,

1612, but the Puritans wanted their own. They did not want to identify with the Separatists from the Church of England. And they wanted a "plain and familiar translation."

The Church of Scotland produced a Psalter in 1564, consisting in part of psalms created in Geneva by the English-speaking refugees. After a series of revisions and new attempts at translation—especially by Francis Rous, 1641—the 1650 *Scottish Psalter* emerged. It is still the authorized version today.

For comparison with *MH* 14 the first two stanzas of the *New Version's* predecessors are printed below:

Old Version, 1562 (1594 edition)

1 O come let us lift up our voice
   and sing unto the Lord:
   In him our rock of health rejoice,
   let us with one accord.

2 Yea, let us come before his face,
   to give him thanks and praise:
   In singing Psalmes unto his grace,
   let us bee glad alwaies.

Bay Psalm Book, 1640

1 O come, let us unto the Lord
   shout loud with singing voyce.
   to the rock of our saving health
   let us make joyfull noyse.

2 Before his presence let us then
   approach with thanksgiving:
   also let us triumphantly
   with Psalmes unto him sing.

Scottish Psalter, 1650

1 O come, let us sing to the Lord:
   come, let us ev'ry one
   A joyful noise make to the Rock
   of our salvation.

2 Let us before his presence come
   with praise and thankful voice;
   Let us sing psalms to him with grace,
   and make a joyful noise.

The *New Version* had ten stanzas for Psalm 95 in 1696; eleven in 1703. Here are the stanzas omitted in *The Mennonite Hymnal:*

Stanza 3, in 1703:
  For God the Lord, enthron'd in state
    Is, with unrival'd Glory, great;
  A king superiour far to all,
    Whom Gods the Heathen falsely call.

Stanza 5 in 1703: 4 in 1696:
  The rouling Ocean's vast Abys
    By the same sov'reign right is his
    (His Maker's liquid empire is) 1696
  'Tis mov'd by his Almighty hand,
    That form'd and fix'd the solid land.

The sign, †, in the text information means that stanza 3 said *"center's wealth"* and *"threat* the skies" in the original edition.

The Mennonite Hymnal has two other psalms from Tate and Brady—*MH* 41 and 285—psalms which are included in many hymnals. To my knowledge *MH 14* is not present in any other hymnal since 1940. But the General Conference Mennonites have included it in all their English language books—1894, 1927, and 1940. The psalm is in the "canon" of many congregations.

SALISBURY appeared first, as far as I can tell, in the *Boston Handel and Haydn Society Collection of Church Music,* first edition, 1822 (where it is spelled SALSBURY), with the name Haydn. Henry Lowell Mason lists it under "Hymn-tune arrangements" in *Hymn-Tunes of Lowell Mason.* [2] He gives 1819 as the date and the *Boston . . . Society,* 1822, as its source. The melody is in the middle of three voices. The bass line has figures to aid the keyboard player in supplying accompanying chords. The hymn has many interesting variations from *The Mennonite Hymnal* form. (See Figure 11.) The triple time came to psalm tunes, perhaps from dances, in the eighteenth century. In fact, the 1708 *Supplement to the New Version* indicated in the introduction how to beat triple time:

  The other sort of time [in addition to duple] you will meet with in this
  Supplement is call'd *Tripla* Time, which is when there are 3 minims (♩)
  in a bar, or one semibreve (♩) and a minim; and the way to keep time to
  such notes is singing two minims with your hand down, and but one up.
  (p. vii)

MH 100 and 152, both in triple time, come from the 1708 book. Other eighteenth-century triple tunes are: common meter—32, 82, 109; long meter—34, 37, 72.

The psalters of the sixteenth and seventeenth centuries often included tunes of the quality that endures through centuries. Thomas Est published *The Whole Booke of Psalmes with their wonted tunes, as they are sung in churches, composed in foure parts . . .* in 1592, with the music

Lord, thou hast known my inmost mind, Thou dost my path and bed inclose; My wak-ing soul on thee relies,

On thee my sleeping thoughts repose: Where from thy presence can I fly, - - - - - Lord, ever present ever nigh?

Figure 11

Boston Handel and Society Collection of Church Music.

arranged in independent parts rather than in open score, as we print it. In his 1594 edition he commented as follows in his presentation to the Keeper of the great *Seal* of England:

The word of God delighteth those which are spiritually minded: the art of music recreateth such, as are not sensually affected: where zeal in the one, and skill in the other do meet, the whole man is revived. . . . Blessed is that man which delighteth therein [in the psalms] and meditateth in the same continually. He that is heavy, hath the Psalms to help his prayer: He that is merry, hath the Psalms to guide his affections; and he that hath a desire to be seriously employed in either of these duties, hath this excellent gift of God the knowledge of music offered him for his further help: that the heart rejoicing in the word, and the ears delighting in the notes and tunes, both these might join together unto the praise of God. Some have pleased themselves with Pastorals, others with Madrigals, but such as are endued with *David's* heart, desire with *David* to sing unto God Psalms and Hymns, and spiritual songs. For whose sake I have set forth this work, that they may busy themselves in the Psalms of this holy man, being by men of skill put into four parts, that each man may sing that part, which best may serve his voice.

It is interesting that some of the composers who "pleased themselves with pastorals . . . and madrigals" also wrote psalm tunes. Within fifty years after the publication of the *Old Version,* 1562, excellent melodies

58

appeared, and they were often arranged by some of the finest composers of the day—Farmer, Dowland, Kirbye, Tallis, and Gibbons. Many of the tunes were in common meter, for example, *MH* 28, 46, 241, 315, and 393. *MH* 246 is in short meter and 496, long meter.

[1] Zolton Haraszti, *The Enigma of the Bay Psalm Book.* Chicago: University of Chicago Press, 1956, p. 6.
[2] Cambridge: Harvard University Press, 1944.

34. Give to Our God Immortal Praise. WARRINGTON.

Isaac Watts (1674-1748) was a young man in his twenties when the *New Version* of the psalms was published. We would expect a revival of interest in singing the psalms in fresh language. But in the preface to his *Hymns and Spiritual Songs,* 1707, he lamented the "dull Indifference, the negligent and the thoughtless Air that sits upon the Faces of a whole Assembly, while the Psalm is on their Lips . . ."

His *Psalms of David Imitated in the Language of the New Testament,* 1719, presented psalms in paraphrase rather than direct translation. He needed to depart from the literal because the psalms seemed to him at times inconsistent with Christian experience. He observed in his 1707 Preface:

Some of 'em are almost opposite to the Spirit of the Gospel: Many of them foreign to the State of the New-Testament, and widely different from the present Circumstances of Christians. Hence it comes to pass, that when spiritual Affections are excited within us, and our souls are raised a little above this Earth in the beginning of a Psalm, we are check'd on a sudden in our Ascent toward Heaven by some Expressions that are more suited to the Days of *Carnal Ordinances,* and fit only to be sung in the *Worldly Sanctuary.* When we are just entring into an Evangelic Frame by some of the Glories of the Gospel presented in the brightest Figures of *Judaism,* yet the very next Line perhaps which the Clerk parcels out unto us, hath something in it so extreamly *Jewish* and cloudy, that darkens our Sight of God the Saviour: Thus by keeping too close to *David* in the House of God, the Vail of *Moses* is thrown over our Hearts. [1]

Twelve of the psalms apparently had the "veil of Moses" thrown over them. Watts omitted Psalms 28, 43, 52, 54, 59, 64, 70, 79, 88, 108, 137, and 140 from his *Psalms of David.* Each of these has a vindictive character in at least a few verses, or speaks of the enemy or evildoers, or of dashing the children against the stones.

Thirteen of the psalms he set in all three of the English psalm meters—
C.M., L.M. and S.M. (1, 2, 8, 23, 32, 36, 45, 63, 73, 90, 95, 117, and 118). *The Mennonite Hymnal* does not have an example of one Watts psalm in all three meters. However, Table 2 below shows that Psalms 23 and 103 appear in two meters in *The Mennonite Hymnal*.

Following is a table of further details of Watts's *Psalms:*

Table 1

Meter	Total number of Psalms set
Common meter C.M.	98
Long Meter L.M.	87 Psalms; two set twice
Short meter S.M.	27
8.8.8.8.8.8.	8
6.6.6.6.4.4.4.4.	4
6.6.8.6.6.8.	3
10.10.10.10.10.10.	2

Watts's *Psalms* in *The Mennonite Hymnal:* Table 2.

Table 2

Psalm number	MH number		Meter
19	220		L.M.
23	63	66	C.M.D. S.M.
36	39		L.M.
39	315		C.M.
46	326		L.M.
63	35		L.M.
72	203		L.M.
84	392		6.6.6.6.4.4.4.4. (or 8.8.)
90	84		C.M.
98	122		C.M.
100	48		L.M.
103	245	72	S.M. L.M.
117	36		L.M.
118	499		C.M.
133	382		S.M. (Watts and Others)
136	34		L.M.
139	79		L.M.
146	25		8.8.8.8.8.8.
147	515		C.M.

Watts began the procedure of paraphrasing in his early works:

I have borrow'd the Sense, and much of the Form of the Song from some particular Portions of Scripture. . . . You will always find in this paraphrase dark Expressions enlighten'd, and the Levitical Ceremonies and Hebrew Forms of Speech chang'd into the Worship of the Gospel, and explain'd in the Language of our Time and Nation; and what would not bear such an Alteration is omitted and laid aside. After this manner should I rejoyce to see a good part of the Book of Psalms fitted for the Use of our Churches, and *David* converted into a Christian. [2]

Thus "Give to our God Immortal Praise" (*MH* 34) is a paraphrase of Psalm 136. This psalm presents twenty-six statements recounting the acts of God in history, always concluding with the refrain, "For his mercy endureth forever." Watts used only eight statements and alternating forms of the refrain:

Wonders of grace to God belong;
Repeat his mercies in your song.

His mercies ever shall endure,
When . . .

The Mennonite Hymnal omitted stanzas 5 and 6 of the eight. They read:

5 The Jews he freed from Pharaoh's Hand,
   And brought them to the promis'd Land:
   Wonders of Grace to God belong,
   Repeat his Mercies in your Song.

6 He saw the Gentiles dead in Sin,
   And felt his Pity work within:
   His mercies ever shall endure,
   When Death and Sin shall reign no more.

These stanzas help to contribute to the progression of God's acts in history. Stanzas 6 and 7 (5 of *MH*) move beyond the Old Testament recitals—Deuteronomy 26:5-11, Joshua 24:1-14, Nehemiah 9:6-31, and Psalms 78, 105, and 106, for example—to God's continuing work in Christ.

Incidentally, a few of the recent folk-like songs of the 1960s and 1970s are built on this biblical formula. The *Ballad of Holy History* by Schultz and Abels [3] says in stanza 18 and 19, "God's mighty acts still happen, So we pray Make this a resurrection day." In a briefer form, *Allelu* by Ray Repp, [4] beginning with prophecy of Christ's birth, suggests that God's acts carry on into our time. In this respect they are patterned after Paul's speech in the synagogue, Acts 13:6-41.

The principle of improvising verses allows for immediate acknowledgement of God's work in the past and present. We could borrow from the Africans and Black Americans the improvising solo-response form, which can carry changing texts. At the 1978 Mennonite World

Conference in Wichita a Kenyan music group sang such a song, incorporating the particular time and place. The approximate notes:

The SOLO (B) section was improvised to incorporate words suitable for the specific occasion. (Translation: 1. Lord, you care for us. 2. Even in our travel. 3. And in the meeting.) This eight-syllable pattern: ♪♪♩♪♪♪♪♩ could carry any number of improvised texts, such as:

He has brought us here together, . . .

For singing and rejoicing, . . .

He led them out of Egypt, . . .

The Kenya Music Team treated it freely, varying the number of syllables from verse to verse. This is similar in flexibility to the Gelineau Psalms (see p. 31). The Swahili song, which actually came to Kenya from South Africa, had several other refrains, which the soloist introduced in SOLO (A): *Bwana, Bwana* (Lord), and *Mungu, Mungu* (God). "Praise Him" would be a suitable English refrain, among many other possibilities.

WARRINGTON, the tune of *MH* 34, was written by Ralph Harrison (1748-1810). He included it in his *Sacred Harmony, or a Collection of Psalm Tunes, Ancient and Modern,* 1784 to 1791. The arrangement was four part with the melody in the tenor and figured bass numbers.

For some reason the tune is not in frequent use in today's hymnals. Archibald Jacob, in *Songs of Praise Discussed,* 1933, gave his opinion of its quality:

The tune is an excellent one, both in form and melody, combining strength and smoothness in a remarkable manner. Its effect is partly due to the satisfactory equipoise of movement by step and leap, the latter being in no case greater than a fourth, thus preserving the flow of the melody while infusing vigour into the whole. (p. 13)

In the introduction to his 1719 Psalter, Watts commented on how to sing. In his day the Clerk "parceled out" the psalm and tune for the benefit of the people who had no books.

Of the Manner of Singing

It were to be wished that all Congregations and private Families would sing as they do in foreign Protestant Countries, without reading Line by Line. Though the Author has done what he could to make the Sense complete in every Line or two, yet many Inconveniences will always attend this unhappy Manner of Singing: But where it cannot be altered, these two Things may give some Relief.

First, Let as many as can do it, bring Psalm-Books with them, and look on the Words while they sing, so far as to make the Sense complete.

Secondly, Let the Clerk read the whole Psalm over aloud, before he begins to parcel out the Lines, that the People may have some Notion of what they sing: and not to be forced to drag on heavily through eight tedious Syllables without any Meaning, till the next Lines come to give the Sense of them.

It were to be wished also, that we might not dwell so long upon every single Note, and draw out the Syllables to such a tiresome Extent, with a constant Uniformity of Time; which disgraces the Music, and puts the Congregation quite out of Breath in singing five or six stanzas: Whereas if the Method of Singing were but reformed to a greater Speed of Pronunciation, we might often enjoy the Pleasure of a longer Psalm, with less Expense of Time and Breath; and our Psalmody would be more agreeable to that of the ancient Churches, more intelligible to others, and more delightful to ourselves.

(p. vii-viii; Introduction called "Advertisement to the Readers.")

The Mennonite Hymnal includes two additional settings of Psalm 136, one from the seventeenth century and the other from the nineteenth. At age 15, John Milton (1608-74) set Psalm 136 to twenty-four stanzas to the meter of the Genevan Psalm 136. It was published in 1645, but 1623 would probably have been a more revealing date to accompany his name at *MH* 70. *The Mennonite Hymnal* uses stanzas 1, 2, 7, and 22, with alterations needed to fit a few of the lines to the meter. Stanzas 8 through 13, omitting the Refrain, will give a fuller view of the narrative character of the long poem:

8 And caus'd the Golden-tressed Sun,
All the day long his cours to run.

9 The horned moon to shine by night,
Amongst her spangled sisters bright.

10 He with his thunder-clasping hand,
[s]Mote the first born of Egypt Land.

11 And in despight of Pharao fell,
He brought from thence his Israel.

12 The ruddy waves he cleft in twain,
Of the Erythraean main.

13 The floods stood still like walls of Glass,
While the Hebrew Bands did pass.

(John Milton, *Poems, both English and Latin,* 1645.)

It might be an interesting exercise to arrange these stanzas in a usable 7.7.

Because the refrain of GENEVA 136 does not end on the keynote but rolls around to the next verse, we suggested concluding with the repetition of stanza 1.

Henry Williams Baker, whose tune STEPHANOS appears at *MH* 230 (see p. 19), versified Psalm 136 for *Hymns Ancient and Modern,* 1861, "Praise, O Praise Our God and King" (*MH* 518). He based his version on Milton's. The last stanza gives praise to the Father, Son, and Holy Spirit, in keeping with the Roman Catholic tradition of singing the doxology at the end of every psalm and canticle. The omitted stanzas follow:

3 And the silver moon by night,
   Shining with her gentle light;
      For His mercies still endure
      Ever faithful, ever sure.

6 Praise Him for our harvest-store,
   He hath filled the garner-floor;
      (Refrain).

7 And for richer Food than this,
   Pledge of everlasting bliss;
      (Refrain).

MONKLAND was written for this text by an organist, John Bernard Wilkes (1785-1869).

[1] Selma L. Bishop, *Isaac Watts Hymns and Spirited Songs.* London: Faith Press, 1962, p. li.
[2] *Ibid.* p. liv-lv.
[3] *Songs for Today.* Minneapolis: American Lutheran Church, 1963.
[4] Los Angeles: F.E.L., 1967.

231-232. I Heard the Voice of Jesus.
KINGSFORD and BONAR.

Horatius Bonar (1808-89) was a minister of the Church of Scotland and later of the Scottish Free Church. He was a prolific writer, not only of hymns, but also of evangelical tracts and devotional books. He was deeply interested in prophecy, and his travels to Egypt and Palestine encouraged his writing in that field.

The Church of Scotland maintained the Calvinist position of psalm singing through most of the nineteenth century. There was no hymnal, only a psalter, until 1898. Organs were not permitted. The arguments voiced in the nineteenth century against their use sound very much like those of the Mennonite Church in the mid-twentieth.[1]

In 1843 a group of dissenters withdrew from the established church which was controlled by the government, and founded the Free Church of Scotland. Bonar joined that body and eventually became the moderator of its General Assembly. The dissenters were freer to use hymns along with the psalms.

Bonar wrote nearly six hundred hymns, many of which remained in use for many years. *The Mennonite Hymnal* has eight: 64, 231-2, 248, 287, 341, 405, 431, and 588. Probably the most famous is "I Heard the Voice of Jesus," published in *Hymns Original and Selected,* 1846, with the title, "The Voice from Galilee." He wrote this and a number of others for the children in his Sunday school. The personal, devotional quality of his hymns relates them in character to the American gospel songs of the last quarter of the century. In fact, Bonar seems to have welcomed Moody and Sankey to Scotland for their visit of 1874. Ira Sankey reported concerning "In the Land of Strangers" (*MH* 588), "Written for me by Dr. Bonar, in 1874, this hymn became the favorite song of the choir of over fifteen hundred voices . . . in Washington during the winter of 1894."[2]

The Mennonite Hymnal has printed Bonar's text with two different tunes, KINGSFORD and BONAR, both published in the early twentieth century, only five years apart. They have the same poetic meter, of course—common meter double. They also have the same pattern of melodic repetitions—*a a' b a'*. The first two 8.6.s begin alike, but the second ends more decisively than the first (*a a'*). The third line presents a contrast (B) to the first two, and the fourth phrase concludes decisively with the music of the second. Thus the form is *a a' b a'*.

However, they do not sound at all alike. The following table compares them:

Area of Comparison	KINGSFORD - Vaughan Williams	BONAR - Brunk
Musical meter	Duple	Triple
Number of rhythmic patterns of Phrases	5	2
Mode	Natural minor	Major
Kinds of cadences or Phrase endings	IV I (fa, doh) or by step, many variations	V I (sol, doh)
Harmonic movement. Number of times keynote is in Bass	E. 10 times	D. 27 times
Style	Folk tune fourteeners (see below)	19th century New England, in the style of Lowell Mason

Duple and triple meter create quite different psychological effects. Duple is based on oppositions, on back-and-forth relationships. (See p.

19.) Triple rolls around, always pushing on to the next measure. Jung gives a psychological explanation for grouping in threes:

> With the appearance of the number two, *another* appears alongside the one, a happening which is so striking that in many languages "the other" and "the second" are expressed by the same word ... The "One," ... seeks to hold its one-and-alone existence, while the "Other" ever strives to be another opposed to the One. The One will not let go of the Other because, if it did, it would lose its character; and the Other pushes itself away from the One in order to exist at all. Thus there arises a tension of opposites between the One and the Other. But every tension of opposites culminates in a release, out of which comes the "third." In the third, the tension is resolved, and the lost unity is restored. [3]

We do not consciously concern ourselves with the psychology of 2s and 3s as we sing, but we are intuitively influenced by the organization.

By observing the rhythmic patterns of phrases, cadences, and the kind of movement in the bass, we can tell that Vaughan Williams was more concerned with variation than was J. D. Brunk. BONAR is the simpler of the two tunes and the more repetitious.

Vaughan Williams used an English folk (or folk-like) tune from a collection, perhaps by Lucy Broadwood. KINGSFOLD has the long phrases of ballad meter, to which Erik Routley refers in the *Music of Christian Hymnody,* in a chapter on Anglo-Genevan Psalmody: "The ballad meter is properly described as the 'fourteener.' The ballad tunes are composed in two or four phrases of fourteen syllables each, and the movement in the mind of the metricist was therefore the free flowing phrase of KINGSFOLD ... rather than the broken-up phrases of the later C.M. psalm tune." [4] (See p. 18 on Vaughan William's arrangements.)

Brunk chose an approach Lowell Mason liked, that of constantly repeating a rhythmic figure· ♩♫ , in this case. He would have expected Mennonites to be familiar with that style. He wrote for four-part unaccompanied singing.

John David Brunk (b. March 13, 1872, in Harrisonburg, Virginia—d. February 5, 1926, Elkhart, Indiana) was an influential music leader of the Mennonite Church in the first quarter of this century. He was trained at the New England Conservatory of Music in Boston and at the American Conservatory in Chicago.

Brunk worked in three areas of music—teaching, hymnal editing, and composition. He taught at Bridgewater College in Virginia, and at Goshen College, where he was director of the School of Music from 1906 to 1914. He also visited many Mennonite congregations to teach music and encourage good hymn singing. His *Educational Vocal Studies* was a method book, in the tradition of the *Harmonia Sacra* of the nineteenth-century singing school, designed for church music leaders.

Brunk was deeply involved in preparing hymnals for the Mennonite Church. At his urging committees were appointed, and the *Church and*

Sunday School Hymnal was published, under his editorship, in 1902. He edited the 1911 *Supplement* to that book in order to extend the usefulness of the book to Sunday schools and young people's meetings. The *Supplement* and *Life Songs,* 1916, introduced more gospel songs than had previous books. Between 1919 and his death he was working on the manuscript for the *Church Hymnal,* which he edited with S. F. Coffman. The book was published in 1927.

I have always marveled at the grace of Brunk and Coffman under the distressing circumstances that accompanied their work on the *Church Hymnal.* It seems that at a mission board meeting, held in Harrisonburg in 1925, a group of church leaders decreed that the new hymnbook should have 150 songs with refrains. In those authoritarian days, the editors adjusted. There are few documents on this issue.[5] On December 9, 1925, Brunk wrote as follows to his committee:

> In order to finish the collection for the new hymnal it was necessary to secure a number of GOSPEL SONG books. I have gathered about 20 or 25 from the various Publishers of such books. It was the plan that another copy of each book which I have was to be sent to some member of the Com. for examination. From these books each member was to make a LIST of the songs in those books which he wished to nominate for a place among the 75 songs with Chorus to complete our List.

Further, in an article for the *Youth's Christian Companion,* "John D. Brunk—His Ideals as a Music Worker for the Mennonite Church," his daughter, Fannie Brunk, wrote in November, 1930:

> The greatest disappointment that he met in his editorial work was having to admit to the New Hymnal a large number of songs that he felt should not go in the book. After his death (Feb. 5, 1926) more of this type of song was added, so the Hymnal as it is today is not Mr. Brunk's ideal of what it should be, although it is indeed a great asset to the church.[6]

I have always attributed the "grayness" of the *Church Hymnal* to that rather high-handed act in 1925. I regret that, as a result, the young people of my generation did not know some of the greatest hymns of the Christian tradition during their childhood.

Brunk carried on the practice, begun in *Hymns and Tunes,* 1890, of writing tunes for the books he compiled. In the *Church and Sunday School Hymnal* there are ten of his tunes; in the *Supplement,* 1911, there are five; in the *Life Songs,* 1916, there are sixteen; in the *Church Hymnal* there are twelve.

There is no J. D. Brunk style. Rather, he seemed interested in writing in the manner Mennonites were currently singing. I see several types:

Type	Example	Comments
1. Chorale like; thick chords	WATTS, *MH* 48 (from 1911)	Compilers of *MH* altered rhythm

2. Victorian; chromatic, changing dynamics	"In Thy Holy Place we Bow" (1911)	
3. Triple psalm-tune type	HAGERSTOWN, *MH* 35 (from 1902)	Tune name from Maryland City, home of Brunk's wife, Mary Kate Martin Brunk
4. Lowell Mason, repeated rhythmic figure	BONAR, *MH* 231 (from 1911)	Cf. NASHVILLE, *MH* 25 and HARWELL, *MH* 201
5. 19th-century Sunday school song	"Ye Are the Light of the World" (1902)	Reminiscent of "What a Friend We Have in Jesus."
6. Gospel song style of 1875 and following	"Alone with Thee" (1927)	

For some reason, the American folk hymn, so prominent in the singing schools, did not seem to interest him. He did not imitate that style, nor did he include many folk tunes in the *Church Hymnal*.

The Mennonite Hymnal retained only three tunes of J. D. Brunk. Many people will miss his "In Thy Holy Place We Bow," with the text by S. F. Coffman. After much reflection and discussion the Text Committee rejected it because of the theological implications for a church that does not call places "holy." We do not have a "sanctuary," nor the accompanying symbols, such as incense. But this hymn was valuable throughout the Mennonite Church. I recommend that those who miss it— or any lost favorite—cut it out of the old book (or get permission to duplicate it) and paste it in the back of *The Mennonite Hymnal*.

Early in the compiling procedures for *The Mennonite Hymnal* the Mennonite Church committee developed a position on original hymns and tunes, based on their examination of materials they had received. They expressed openness to their own writers and composers and pledged to read their work. They agreed that "the inclusion of Mennonite materials should be based on the integrity of those materials—their right to be in a hymnal."[7] They were not committed to using all the hymns and tunes submitted, but "the hymnal should include several Mennonite works."[8] Although the joint committee did not articulate its principle in writing, they reached and operated by a similar agreement.

As a result, *The Mennonite Hymnal* has few Mennonite texts or tunes. Many of J. D. Brunk's tunes, for example, had momentary value. Brunk tried, successfully, to reach the church's taste at a particular time in history. Forty years later the compilers dropped those which they judged to have passed their usefulness. Many of the new materials submitted seemed also to belong to a past era.

[1] In 1808 a debate on "The Organ Question" between a Dr. Ritchie and Dr.

Porteous was reported in the Proceedings of the Presbytery of Glasgow. Dr. Ritchie argued that if David's instruments had been "a gross profanation of sacred things," Jesus would not have been silent on the subject. Paul never warned against the harp, and John included it in Revelation. Dr. Porteous answered that the Church of Scotland cannot go back to "an Infant Church": they are bound to defend existing practice. He found in the New Testament "no vestige of authority for the use of instruments." The debate was reported in 1856 by Robert S. Candlish, who was concerned about the "recent movement on behalf of instruments."

[2] Sankey's *Story of the Gospel Hymns.* Philadelphia: Sunday School Times, 1906, p. 245.

[3] C. J. Jung, *Psychology and Religion: West and East.* New York: Pantheon, 1958, pp. 8-9.

[4] London: Independent Press, 1957, p. 37.

[5] I have this by oral tradition. When I mentioned this event at a committee meeting in 1964 or 1965, C. K. Lehman recalled that he had been appointed to join the compilers to help expedite the wishes of the leaders.

[6] This paragraph was omitted from the article, printed in the *YCC,* May 31, 1931, pp. 588-9.

[7] From the Minutes of December 26-28, 1963, p. 5.

[8] *Ibid.*

295. Hope of the World. GENEVA 12.

Georgia Harkness (1891-1974), was a distinguished Methodist theologian and educator. She received her education at Cornell, Boston, and Harvard universities. She was the first woman to hold a full professorship in an American seminary—Garrett Biblical Institute in Evanston, Illinois, in 1939. She was also professor of applied theology at Pacific School of Religion in Berkeley, California, until her retirement in 1961.

Dr. Harkness was an ordained Methodist minister and was influential in that church's granting, in 1956, full clergy rights to women. She was a pacifist, who helped formulate a position on war and peace which was adopted by the Methodist General Conference. [1]

"Hope of the World" *MH* 295, was her response to a request sent out by the Hymn Society of America for hymns suitable for singing at the Second Assembly of the World Council of Churches, to be held in Evanston in 1954. The directions specified the use of one or both of the themes chosen for the Evanston meeting: the Church's oneness in Christ, and Christ, the Hope of the World. Authors were also asked to write in well-known meters used in standard hymnals.

Nearly five hundred hymns were submitted from six different countries. "Hope of the World" was the first choice of the judges. It was printed in a booklet of *Eleven Ecumenical Hymns,* all responses to the Hymn Society's search.

"God of the Fertile Fields," *MH* 360, another of Harkness's winners in a Hymn Society contest, was written for use at the Quadrennial National Methodist Town and Country Conference, held in Bloomington, Indiana, in June 1955. It was published in *Fourteen New Rural Hymns,* 1955.[2]

"Hope of the World" was printed with two tunes—ANCIENT OF DAYS:

and DONNE SECOURS (GENEVA 12), *MH* 295. The introductory page in *Eleven Ecumenical Hymns* includes these sentences concerning the music: "New hymns naturally suggest the possibility of new tunes; and the Hymn Society invites the submitting of new tunes for use with these new texts."

Is it the old tunes that make these texts sound old also? Although they are graceful, they seem to point to the past. Often hymn contests bring a flood of uninspiring pieces. Entries seem to be first attempts of aspiring poets. That is not the case, of course, with Georgia Harkness, who had practiced the craft of writing for many years and had published three books of verse between 1935 and 1953.

But the limitations of the form make lively hymn writing difficult in the twentieth century. In the first place, language has been undergoing a drastic change in the last few decades. The King James Version of the Bible, which was the model for fine English for three and a half centuries, is being supplanted by many modern translations. Liturgies are modernized as well; for example, the pronoun "you" replacing "thou" appearing in prayers and folk hymns. The religious language of most of our hymns is gradually sounding archaic. Although a congregation can borrow language from many historical periods for use in worship, poets need to write in their own idiom for an honest result.

Second, but less important, the form of the hymn is dated. Ballad meter, for example, was lively for Thomas Sternhold and his friends in Henry VIII's court. Poets now have to find the comparable forms that encourage spontaneous expression.

Hymns, in the third place, must fulfill their function. They must be usable by persons who are not specialists in either poetry or music. They must be singable by groups of persons whose culture does not encourage active music making. The good poet presents a text with several potential levels of meaning.

The most recent request from the Hymn Society of America—for new psalms—brought this encouraging poem, published in *The Hymn,* April, 1979, p. 128:

Creating God, your fingers trace
The bold designs of farthest space;
Let sun and moon and stars and light
And what lies hidden praise your might.

Sustaining God, your hands uphold
Earth's mysteries known or yet untold;
Let water's fragile blend with air,
Enabling life, proclaim your care.

Redeeming God, your arms embrace
All now oppressed for creed or race;
Let peace, descending as the dove,
Make known on earth your healing love.

Indwelling God, your gospel claims
One family with a billion names;
Let every life be touched by grace
Until we praise you face to face.

The fact that it was written on this side of the language revolution and twenty years after "Hope of the World" shows up in the freshness of imagery and the everyday language of the 1970s. Its long meter presents a traditional framework. Jeffery W. Rowthorn, the author of this paraphrase of Psalm 148, in 1974, is a member of the faculty of Yale University's Divinity School and Institute of Sacred Music. He is an Anglican clergyman.

The compilers of *The Mennonite Hymnal* chose GENEVA 12 for "Hope of the World." The fine Genevan tune goes back far enough before the nineteenth century that it has a "new" sound for many people, particularly in its original rhythmic form. (See pp. 28, 34-35 for historical aspects of Genevan tunes and for the treatment of rests.)

Coincidentally, one of the newest tunes in *The Mennonite Hymnal*—new in sound as well as date of composition—is also in 11.10.11.10. meter. *MH* 616, CITY OF GOD, by Daniel Moe (b. 1926), is a fine tune that fits rather well with "Hope of the World." The 1957 tune brings freshness to the 1954 text. CITY OF GOD was written for another Hymn Society text, "O Jesus Christ, to Thee May Hymns Be Rising," by Bradford Gray Webster.[3]

[1] Deborah C. Loftis, "The Hymns of Georgia Harkness," *The Hymn*, October, 1977, pp. 186-191.

[2] 1953 seems to be an error in *The Mennonite Hymnal*.

[3] Published in *Five New Hymns On the City,* for a Convention on Urban Life in America, Columbus, Ohio, 1954.

228. I Sought the Lord. FAITH.

"I Sought the Lord" is an anonymous text which comes from *The Pilgrim Hymnal,* 1904. It appeared earlier in *Holy Songs, Carols, and Sacred Ballads,* 1880, published in Boston by Robert Brothers, though some hymnals give an earlier date without documentation.

The meter is unusual. We have a number of 10.10.10.10. hymns, but 10.10.10.6. is unique in *The Mennonite Hymnal.* It is quite unusual, in fact, in any hymnbook.

Often a tune will settle with a given text and function as a proper tune, wedded to that particular text. For example, EIN FESTE BURG always goes with "A Mighty Fortress Is our God"; NICAEA fits "Holy, Holy, Holy," and so on. "I Sought the Lord" has no proper tune. It is often combined with the first half of a Genevan psalm tune, with a bit of alteration. In other hymnals it is accompanied by several nineteenth-century Romantic tunes and others of a folk-like character. The compilers of *The Mennonite Hymnal* decided to add to the tunes borrowed or written for this text and invited Harold Moyer to compose a new tune.

Harold Moyer had worked with the compilation from the beginning of the venture. He had welcomed the assignment of making four-part arrangements of American folk tunes we had found in the singing school books. But to write a new tune seemed to him more difficult than writing a symphony—a project he had recently completed for his doctorate in composition from the University of Iowa.

He commented on his concern to write in an idiom that genuinely interested him and at the same time to provide music which Mennonites could honestly enjoy singing. The four-part, unaccompanied style of many Mennonite congregations presented severe limitations, but he agreed to try a setting.

In the tune, FAITH, he worked imaginatively within the limitations. He used the natural minor scale, rejecting the chromatic effects of the Romantic period found in a tune like REST, "Dear Lord and Father of Mankind," for example. In the Moyer tune there is variety in texture and rhythmic patterns. The tune wears well.

J. Harold Moyer (b. 1927), Professor of Music at Bethel College, North Newton, Kansas, commented on writing his tune, FAITH:

In the mid-twentieth century composers found some difficulty in choosing an authentic musical style for writing hymn tunes. The choices seemed to be an older nineteenth-century idiom, or a newer type of melody and harmony which would be difficult for congregational use. In this tune I have tried to combine freshness with practicality. It was written in 1965 during meetings of the Joint Hymnal Committee at Goshen.

Another hymn in a similar position to "I Sought the Lord"—composed by a Mennonite and used appreciatively—is "I Bind My Heart," *MH* 353.

Here we have another text with a strange meter—6.7.7.7., not present in most hymnals. The compilers asked several composers to submit tunes; UNION was chosen. The composer, J. Randall Zercher (b. 1940), is a member of the music faculty of Hesston College, Hesston, Kansas. He too chose to use the natural minor scale and varied textures (at times two of the voices join in unison). The spacing of the upper and lower voices is unusual in the third phrase, and the ending is even more surprising. Most groups include the Amen[1] to bring the basses back to the keynote. The tune, UNION, was named for the composer's recent marriage, for the joining of two Mennonite groups to make a hymnal, and for the seminary where he had just completed his master's degree.

[1] The Mennonite Church had only occasional hymns ending in Amen in the *Church Hymnal*, 1927. It seems that Amens were not planned editorially, but they were carried over from the sources the editors used. On the other hand, the General Conference Mennonites in the *Mennonite Hymnary*, 1940, had an Amen on practically every hymn, though the editors comment that their use is optional. Both groups wanted to compromise between the two positions for the 1969 book and asked Coeditor Lester Hostetler to plan the placement of Amens. He attached them to most hymns of prayer and praise.

There are still widely differing opinions on their use. In certain circles Amens are eliminated because their liturgical origin called for an affirming response from the congregation to something they had heard; the congregation should not be affirming its own statement. Elsewhere the congregation's particular tradition is strong; a hymn may not seem finished without the Amen. Certainly congregations should be free to work out their own approach. The written page is not absolute.

552. There Were Ninety and Nine.
NINETY AND NINE.

Ira D. Sankey (1840-1908) gives the background to "The Ninety and Nine" in his *Story of the Gospel Hymns*. He discovered Elizabeth Clephane's poem in a newspaper as he and Dwight L. Moody (1837-99) were traveling by train from Glasgow to Edinburgh to evangelistic meetings in 1874. The text impressed him so much that he cut it out and placed it in his musical scrapbook, which, he said, "has been the seed-plot from which sprang many of the gospel songs that are known throughout the world."[1] He reported:

At the noon meeting on the second day [in Edinburgh] . . . the subject presented by Mr. Moody and other speakers was "The Good Shepherd." When Mr. Moody had finished speaking he called upon Dr. Bonar to say a few words. He spoke only a few minutes, but with great power, thrilling the immense audience by his fervid eloquence. At the conclusion of Dr. Bonar's words Mr. Moody turned to me with the question, "Have you a solo appropriate for this subject, with which to close the service?" I had nothing suitable in mind, and was greatly troubled to know what to do. The Twenty-third Psalm occurred to me, but this had been sung several times in the meeting. I knew that every Scotchman in the audience would join me if I sang that, so I could not possibly render this favorite psalm as a solo. At this moment I seemed to hear a voice saying: "Sing the hymn you found on the train!" But I thought this impossible, as no music had ever been written for that hymn. Again the impression came strongly upon me that I must sing the beautiful and appropriate words I had found the day before, and placing the little newspaper slip on the organ in front of me, I lifted my heart in prayer, asking God to help me so to sing that the people might hear and understand. Laying my hands upon the organ I struck the key of A flat, and began to sing.

Note by note the tune was given, which has not been changed from that day to this. As the singing ceased a great sigh seemed to go up from the meeting, and I knew that the song had reached the hearts of my Scotch audience. Mr. Moody was greatly moved. Leaving the pulpit, he came down to where I was seated. Leaning over the organ, he looked at the little newspaper slip from which the song had been sung, and with tears in his eyes said: "Sankey, where did you get that hymn? I never heard the like of it in my life." I was also moved to tears and arose and replied: "Mr. Moody, that's the hymn I read to you yesterday on the train, which you did not hear." Then Mr. Moody raised his hand and pronounced the benediction, and the meeting closed. Thus "The Ninety and Nine" was born. [2]

Sankey tells stories of the transforming effect of this hymn on people throughout the world—in England, France, the United States, South Africa, and in a Spanish-speaking country of South America. The song spread rapidly through his *Sacred Songs and Solos*.

One usually unsympathetic critic recognized its power. He described Sankey's appearance at the harmonium:

It was inexpressively ludicrous to behold. Rolling his eyes in an affected manner, he touched a few simple chords, and then a marvelous transformation came over the room. In a sweet, powerful voice, with an exquisite simplicity combined with irresistible emotion, he sang. "There were Ninety and Nine!" The man was transfigured. A deathly hush came over the room, and I felt my eyes fill with tears. [3]

"The Ninety and Nine" and many other songs which emerged with the Moody-Sankey revivals owed their strength to their simplicity and folk-like character. The harshest critics found them simple to the point of banality. But Robert M. Stevenson, informed by his knowledge of church history and observation of the church's experience with gospel songs, said in 1953:

Gospel hymnody has the distinction of being America's most typical contribution to Christian song. Gospel hymnody has been a plough digging up the hardened surfaces of pavemented minds. Its very obviousness has been its strength. Where delicacy or dignity can make no impress, gospel hymnody stands up triumphing. In an age when religion must win mass approval in order to survive, in an age when religion must at least win a majority vote from the electorate, gospel hymody is inevitable. Sankey's songs are true folk music of the people. Dan Emmett and Stephen Foster only did in secular music what Ira D. Sankey and P. P. Bliss did as validly and effectively in sacred music. [4]

The battle for and against gospel songs has continued among Mennonites throughout the twentieth century. I grew up in a milieu opposed to them and for a number of years crusaded against them. I am grateful to have worked on compiling a hymnal, a job which challenges positions and attitudes toward the shaping of tastes. I am now friendly toward gospel songs. I also observe the disastrous effects on Christians of other cultures when the "devotional, worshipful hymn" is imposed as an absolute.

In Sankey's time, gospel hymns were remarkably functional. They worked in a crowd. Perhaps this was due in part to Moody's personality. He was, by his own admission and reports from his family, quite unmusical—unable to distinguish tones or evaluate a hymn. But he was extremely sensitive to the psychological impact of music on masses of people. "He must see it tried in a crowd, and could discover in an instant its adaptation to awaken feelings which he needed to have in action. If it had the right ring he used it for all it was worth." [5]

Musicians often reject the gospel songs as a tool used to manipulate the crowd. I suspect that it would be useful to get the perspective of other times and places. Since the fifteenth century, our culture has tended to isolate the arts, viewing them as valid for their own sake, thus making the use of the arts as means to ends seem degrading. Traditional African cultures often have no word in their languages like "art" or "music." Rather, the words incorporate the function as well; function is inseparable from the concrete work. Achebe's mask carver comes to mind when I read that Moody must see music "tried in a crowd." Edogo (see p. 47) could not judge the worth of his mask until he saw it in action.

The sudden outburst of gospel-song publications was a phenomenon in itself. Sankey's *Sacred Songs and Solos,* a 24-page booklet, published in England in 1873, was expanded to 1200 songs by 1903. Sankey joined P. P. Bliss, who had published *Gospel Songs* in 1874, to produce *Gospel Hymns and Sacred Songs* in 1875. Books continued to appear: *Gospel Hymns No. 2* in 1876, *No. 3* in 1878, *No. 4* in 1883, *No. 5* in 1887, *No. 6* in 1891. *Gospel Hymns Nos. 1-6 Complete* came in 1894.

In 1890 Mennonite books had a few gospel songs (see p. 25). The 1902, 1911, and 1916 books of the Mennonite Church gradually increased the proportion. The 1927 *Church Hymnal* contained approximately 135 gospel songs out of 657 hymns, though for some reason none were by Sankey. The *Mennonite Hymn Book* of 1927 had approximately 27 out of its 411 total. The *Mennonite Hymnary,* 1940, had about 55 out of 618 hymns.[6] Three by Sankey—"I Have a Savior," "The Ninety and Nine," and "O Safe to the Rock"—were included. The compilers of *The Mennonite Hymnal* chose to revive Sankey songs as strong and historically important examples of the type. In addition to "The Ninety and Nine," *The Mennonite Hymnal* includes: 563, 569, 575, 587, 588, and 589.

A number of the poems of Elizabeth Cecilia Clephane, who spent much of her life in Melrose, Scotland, were published in *Family Treasure,* 1872-74. She wrote "Beneath the Cross of Jesus," *MH* 171, as well as "The Ninety and Nine."

[1] Philadelphia: The Sunday School Times Co., 1906, p. 220.

[2] *Ibid.,* pp. 220-21.

[3] Quoted in *D. L. Moody,* by Gamaliel Bradford, New York: George H. Doran 1927, p. 172.

[4] In *Patterns of Protestant Church Music,* Chapel Hill: Duke University Press, 1953, p. 162.

[5] Bradford, p. 168.

[6] The numbers must be qualified because of the difficulty of the definition of gospel songs. I used a narrow, historical guideline—1875 and beyond (a few back to 1870), many, but not all, with refrains, a tendency toward an evangelistic function in the text, and very simple chords. Often I could not make sharp distinctions between the gospel song and the Sunday school song immediately preceding.

89. The Lord is King, O Praise His Name. SO LANGE JESUS BLEIBT.

The compilers of *The Mennonite Hymnal* borrowed this hymn from the Mennonite Brethren who came from Russia in the 1920s and settled in Canada. This group of immigrants brought with them a German-language hymnody with simple, folk-like tunes. Ben Horch, of Winnipeg, calls that reservoir of several hundred songs which are at the heart of the Mennonite Brethren heritage *Kernlieder* (core songs):

> *Kernlieder* are a part of the oral history of our congregational song that was characterized by rote singing in the congregations, improvisation and an almost intuitive disregard for any consideration regarding authenticity.[1]

The attribution *Choralbuch der Mennoniten* . . . at *MH* 89 is not accurate because that was a book of texts only—no tunes. SO LANGE JESUS BLEIBT was the accepted tune in the oral tradition in Russia and its oral use continued in Canada. As congregations sang it in four parts they gradually altered the harmonies. Horch described the work of the committee appointed to compile the *Gesangbuch*, in 1955:

A wide cross section of the Mennonite constituency . . . improvised four-part congregational singing from the time the first Russlander Mennonites came to Canada in the early 20s to 1955. It was a period when there was no hymn book. . . . [The committee] was persistently diligent to record the harmonies *improvised* by the corporate musical ear of the congregation.[2]

They found written versions but, "what we were concerned about was the importance of an oral tradition of the religious lay brotherhood."[3]

The Mennonite Hymnal used the musical form published in the Mennonite Brethren *Gesangbuch* and published again with English translations in 1959. The General Conference Mennonites of Canada have included SO LANGE JESUS BLEIBT in their *Gesangbuch*, 1942, and again in *Gesangbuch der Mennoniten*, 1965. The bass line from both traditions shows the difference between the written and oral forms. It is especially striking at*:

Not every musical setting of the Mennonite Brethren *Gesangbuch* was adjusted to oral practice, but all the tunes were examined. This represents a procedure quite different from that of *The Mennonite Hymnal*. For compiling *The Mennonite Hymnal* it was essential to present a written form in order to draw together varied traditions that merged in the 1969 book. But there is an interesting difference in philosophy, as well. Ben Horch explained that adjusting to improvised changes keeps a congregation singing "contemporized" versions. He sees in *The Mennonite Hymnal* collection the result of a search for authentic sources.

A more extreme transformation through oral transmission took place with "O Have You Not Heard of That Beautiful Stream," *MH* 556. The Mennonite Brethren *Gesangbuch*, 1955, includes THE BEAUTIFUL STREAM in duple rather than triple time (as found in *The Mennonite Hymnary* and *The Mennonite Hymnal*). The original was $\frac{6}{4}$ rather than $\frac{3}{4}$, but *triple*. The $\frac{4}{4}$ meter changes its character radically (see pp. 65-66). Ben Horch quoted comments of Cornelius Klassen, whom he described as "our only link with history of congregational song in the Mennonite Brethren Church in Russia and its continuance in Canada today":

It can be reasoned that when the Mennonite Brethren church evolved out of and away from the original Mennonite church in Russia, through an outreach ministry by German Baptist evangelists from America, a rote version in $\frac{4}{4}$ time resulted from Gebhardt's beautiful translation from English into German. If this be so, it is possible that a $\frac{4}{4}$ version, ... besides the one in the MB *Gesangbuch,* could conceivably be found in some of the early hymnbooks of these German Baptist evangelists. We doubt whether this will ever be researched as it ought to be. One other reason for the $\frac{4}{4}$ meter ... that suggests itself to our thinking is that any metre in triple time that has the potential of a waltz was, and still is, suspect among Mennonite Brethren as might also be the attitude of the pietist poet Gebhardt. [4]

The Mennonite Brethren liked the German version of this American camp meeting song so well that they had it retranslated back to English (by Peter Klassen, b. 1926), treating the German translation as the original text. It appears in the Mennonite Brethren *Worship Hymnal*, 1971. The refrain reads:

O come to this beautiful stream,
So deep and so fully it flows!
Its waters so free are flowing for thee
Come now, O sinner be free!

Nicolaus Ludwig von Zinzendorf, the author of "The Lord Is King, O Praise His Name" (1700-60), was a "Saxon nobleman and Lutheran Pietist, ... [who] sheltered exiles from Moravia in 1722 in the renewal of the *Unitas Fratrum* in Herrnhut." [5]

His education ... at Halle and the University of Wittenberg impressed a strong sense of Pietism on his receptive spirit. His intention in encouraging the renewal of the Moravian Church in 1722 was not to found another denomination, but to form a "church within a church" to promote brotherhood among all Christians. He was a gifted hymnist, with a remarkable ability to extemporize hymns at the moment of need. [6]

He wrote over two thousand hymns, some of which entered the English-speaking church through John Wesley's translations of the late 1730s. They tend to reveal a warm, personal faith and often a deep awareness of the sufferings of Christ.

Esther Bergen (b. 1921) made the translation of *So lange Jesus bleibt der Herr*—"The Lord Is King"—for the English version (1960) of the Canadian Mennonite Brethren *Gesangbuch,* 1955. One hundred twenty-two of her translations are in the 1960 book, and fifteen of the German versions for the sixty-three songs of the Mennonite World Conference *International Songbook* [7] are hers.

The Mennonite Hymnal includes two other Zinzendorf texts—"Jesus, Still Lead On" (*MH* 319), translated by Jane L. Borthwick (1813-97) and "Heart with Loving Heart United" (*MH* 386), translated by Walter Klaassen for the 1969 book. The latter, which has come into widespread use among Mennonites as a strong statement on the fellowship of believers, is the only hymn in *The Mennonite Hymnal* which addresses God as "You."

[1] From a letter from Ben Horch, June 11, 1979. (In classical German hymnody the term *Kernlieder* refers to a select body of high quality, time-honored hymns which are contained in the main sections of the various evangelical and Reformed German hymnals. *Editor*)

[2] From a letter, June 28, 1979.

[3] *Ibid.*

[4] June 11, 1979.

[5] John H. Giesler, *et al., Moravian Hymns and Chorales*, Winston-Salem: The Moravian Music Foundation, 1978, p. 7.

[6] *Ibid.*, p. 21.

[7] Lombard: MWC, 1978.

294. On Jordan's Stormy Banks I Stand. BOUND FOR THE PROMISED LAND.

In 1800 a religious revival began in Logan County, Kentucky, and spread rapidly through Kentucky, Tennessee, the Carolinas, and soon throughout the United States. Large crowds of people brought covered wagons or tents to the temporary camps of itinerant preachers. A new type of song emerged to express the exuberant spirit of the meetings. In 1915 Louis Benson described the songs of the revival:

. . . with the tumultuous enthusiasm that soon developed, the old hymns were felt to be too sober to express the overwrought feelings of the preacher and the throng. Spontaneous song became a marked characteristic of the camp meetings. Rough and irregular couplets or stanzas were concocted out of Scripture phrases and everyday speech, with liberal interspersing of Hallelujahs and refrains. Such ejaculatory hymns were frequently started by an excited auditor during the preaching, and taken up by the throng, until the meeting dissolved into a "singing-ecstasy" culminating in a general hand-shaking. Sometimes they were given forth by a preacher, who had a sense of rhythm, under the excitement of his preaching and the agitation of his audience. Hymns were also composed more deliberately out of meeting, and taught to the people or lined out from the pulpit. . . .

[The resulting hymn] is individualistic, and deals with the rescue of a sinner: sometimes in direct appeal to "sinners," "backsliders," or "mourners"; sometimes by reciting the terms of salvation; sometimes as a narrative of personal experience for his warning or encouragement. . . . The literary form of the Camp Meeting Hymn is that of the popular ballad or song, in plainest everyday language and of careless or incapable technique. The refrain or chorus is perhaps the predominant feature, not always connected with the subject-matter of the stanza, but rather ejaculatory. In some instances such a refrain was merely tacked on to a familiar hymn or an arrangement of one.[1]

The familiar hymns to which refrains were "tacked on" were often those of Watts and the Wesleys. Watts had explained in his preface to *Hymns and Spiritual Songs,* 1707, that he was aiming toward clarity and simplicity of speech:

I have seldom permitted a Stop in the middle of a Line, and seldom left the end of a Line without one, to comport a little with the unhappy Mixture of Reading and Singing, which cannot presently be reformed. The Metaphors are generally sunk to the Level of vulgar Capacities. I have aimed at ease of Numbers and smoothness of Sound, and endeavour'd to make the sense plain and obvious.[2]

George Pullen Jackson commented that,

this start from the ground, this hymnodic democracy, was doubtless the basis of the subsequent enormous popularity of the Watts manner of hymn; and John and Charles Wesley, whose life activity was in the middle decades of the eighteenth century, brought religious hymnody still nearer to the masses by endowing it with the elements of personal emotion, spiritual spontaneity, and evangelism.[3]

Watts's "Alas and Did My Savior Bleed," *MH* 170, was used repeatedly in camp meetings. Other English hymns were prominent as well. "Jesus, My All, to Heaven Is Gone," by John Cennick, a Moravian minister, and "Come Thou Fount of Every Blessing," *MH* 310, by Baptist Robert Robinson, were favorites, along with "On Jordan's Stormy Banks I

80

Stand," the subject of this essay.

"On Jordan's Stormy Banks" appeared first in Rippon's *A Selection of Hymns from the Best Authors, intended to be an Appendix to Dr. Watts Psalms and Hymns,* 1787. It was titled "The Promised Land." The author, Samuel Stennet (1727-95), was an English Baptist whose hymns (see *MH* 187, "Majestic Sweetness") came to America through John Rippon's important collection. Stanzas 2 and 5 are omitted in *The Mennonite Hymnal*:

2 O the transporting rapturous Scene,
    That rises to my Sight!
Sweet Fields array'd in living green,
    And Rivers of Delight!

5 No chilling Winds, or poisonous Breath,
    Can reach that healthful Shore:
Sickness and Sorrow, Pain, and Death
    Are felt and fear'd no more.

"On Jordan's Stormy Banks" along with the other hymns listed above, formed a type which Ellen Jane Lorenz calls the "mother hymn" to which refrains may be added or "interrupting refrains" interpolated.[4] The refrain of *MH* 294 comes from Miss M. Durham of Georgia. Another Georgian, a Primitive Baptist preacher, Edmund Dumas, added the refrain,

We'll stem the storm, it won't be long;
The heav'nly port is nigh;
We'll stem the storm, it won't be long;
We'll anchor by and by.[5]

J. T. White's version, No. 117 in *Sacred Harp,* 1844, has an interrupting phrase as well as a refrain. His additions are italicized.

On Jordan's stormy banks I stand,
And cast a wishful eye,
    On the other side of Jordan, hallelujah!
To Canaan's fair and happy land,
Where my possessions lie,
    On the other side of Jordan, hallelujah!
REFRAIN:
On the other side of Jordan, hallelujah!
On the other side of Jordan, hallelujah!

The tune for "On Jordan's Stormy Banks," is called PROMISED LAND in *The Southern Harmony,* one of the most important oblong[6] tune books of the nineteenth century. A Baptist, William Walker, compiled the collection and contributed thirty-five of his own tunes. Although PROMISED LAND is attributed to Miss M. Durham, we do not know whether she collected, supplied, or arranged it. The tune undoubtedly existed for a number of years before its appearance in musical notation. It would have spread through the revival meetings by oral means and thus experienced continuous variations of text and music. *The Southern Harmony* version is in the natural minor mode, though by adding a sharp to D in the alto in *MH* 294, Harold Moyer changed it to harmonic minor. The Southern Baptists use its major form:[7]

In *Southern Harmony* the melody of PROMISED LAND lies in the tenor, the middle of three voices. (See Fig. 12.) Notes appear in four shapes—◇ me, ◣ faw, ○ sol, □ law. The first section of the book, which deals with the "Rudiments of Music," shows how to read the treble clef notes, using only four shapes:

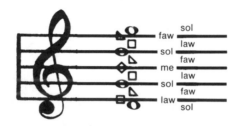

Joseph Funk's *Genuine Church Music,* published three years earlier in the Shenandoah Valley of Virginia, had appeared with three voices and four shapes also. The next essay will deal further with that Mennonite parallel to *Southern Harmony.*

Two other songs in *The Mennonite Hymnal* have characteristics of the camp-meeting song. One is "I Will Arise and Go to Jesus," *MH* 243. Its title was "The Prodigal Son" in P. P. Bliss's *Gospel Songs,* 1874. At that time *gospel song* was a new term and the camp-meeting movement was waning. Philip Bliss (1838-76) said that the number was "furnished by S. H. Price," and he appended the following note to the text and tune:

This chorus may be sung after each of the following stanzas, or as a response to "Come ye Sinners, poor and needy," "Jesus sought me when a stranger," etc. It is one of the old-fashioned, camp-meeting "Spirituals," and well deserves a place among "GOSPEL SONGS." P. P. B.

On Jordan's stormy banks I stand, And cast a wish - ful eye, To Canaan's fair and happy land, Where my possessions lie. I am

bound for the pro - mised land, I'm bound for the pro - mised land, O, who will come and go with me? I am bound for the promised land.

Figure 12

The Southern Harmony
Edited by Glenn C. Wilcox.
Los Angeles: A Pro Musicamericana Reprint, 1966, p. 51. (Reprint of the 1854 edition of *The Southern Harmony.*)

RESTORATION (I WILL ARISE), like PROMISED LAND, emerged first in written form in *Southern Harmony, 1835.* It carried a John Newton text, "Mercy, O Thou Son of David," without a refrain.

Jackson, in *Spiritual Folk-Songs of Early America*[8] pointed out that certain melodic formulas recur frequently in revival spirituals with only insignificant variations, leading him to view folk tunes in families. "I will arise" is one of six basic families with a number of melodic variations. He traced the type back to several secular tunes, with texts like "The Bird Song," "Oh, Love It Is a Killing Thing," "When I First Left Old Ireland," and "The Cruel Mother."[9]

The second camp-meeting type of song is "Come, We That Love the Lord," *MH* 529. The Watts text, from his *Hymns and Spiritual Songs,* 1707, had ten stanzas, of which *The Mennonite Hymnal* incorporates 1, 3, 9, and 10. The refrain is in the camp-meeting tradition in the addition it provides to the "mother hymn." Robert Lowry (1826-99), a Baptist minister and professor, supplied the text for the refrain and wrote the tune. He followed William Bradbury's lead in writing and publishing Sunday school songs and joined with William Howard Doane in producing gospel songbooks. *MH* 355, 573, and 578 are his tunes, and the text-and-tune combination at 567 is his. The character of his tunes is no longer camp meeting—aside from the added refrain—but a precise distinction between Sunday-school and gospel-song styles is not possible.

[1] *The English Hymn. Its Development and Use in Worship.* Reprint: Richmond: John Knox Press, 1962, pp. 292-93.

[2] Selma Bishop. *Isaac Watts. Hymns and Spiritual Songs, 1707-1748.* London: The Faith Press, 1962, pp. liii and liv.

[3] *White Spirituals of the Southern Uplands.* Originally 1933; Reprint: New York: Dover, 1965, p. 214. Between 1933 and his death in 1953, Jackson produced exhaustive studies of the revival spiritual and folk hymns of the South. Several of his books, which include both texts and tunes, are reprinted by Dover. Incidentally, his interest in folk idioms led him to study Amish singing. See "The Strange Music of the Old Order Amish," *Music Quarterly* 35 (July, 1945), pp. 275-88.

[4] Ellen Jane Lorenz's work on northern camp-meeting songs carries on the pioneering work of her grandfather, E. S. Lorenz, *Practical Church Music,* 1909, *MH* 528, and complements Jackson's studies on southern hymnody. Her *Glory Hallelujah! The Story of the Camp-Meeting Spiritual* was published by Abingdon in 1980.

[5] Jackson, pp. 219-20.

[6] See Fig. 13 for the format of a New England oblong tune book. "Oblong" refers to the fact that the horizontal dimension is longer than the vertical dimensions of the book, as is usual. Many of the southern books of camp-meeting and folk tunes were oblong.

[7] *Baptist Hymnal.* Nashville: Convention Press, 1975, No. 490.

[8] First in 1937; reprint New York: Dover, 1964, p. 14.

[9] *Ibid.,* p. 233.

357. Take Up Thy Cross, the Saviour Said. KEDRON.

"Take Up Thy Cross" is the one hymn by which we remember Charles William Everest (1814-77), the rector of an Episcopal church near New Haven, Connecticut. It was written in 1833 and published that year in *Visions of Death and Other Poems.* This was one of the few American hymns included in the English *Hymns Ancient and Modern,* 1861 (No. 165), which used also its sixth verse, the doxology:

To Thee, great Lord, the ONE IN THREE,

All praise for evermore ascend;

O grant us in our home to see

The heavenly life that knows no end.

The text appears in a number of slightly different forms. The sign ‡ should follow the author's name in *The Mennonite Hymnal* because there are several alterations. The most striking is in the second line of stanza 4, where the original was, "And calmly sin's *wild deluge have*" (or *brave,* or *bear*). Handbook writers differ in their understanding of what the author actually wrote.

Perhaps the most interesting of alterations is that in the *Lutheran Book of Worship,* 1978, number 398. One of the goals of its committee was "to bring the language of prayer and praise into conformity with the best current usages."[1]

"Take up your cross," the Savior said,
"If you would my disciple be;
Forsake the past, and come this day,
And humbly follow after me."

Take up your cross, let not its weight
Pervade your soul with vain alarm;
His strength shall bear your spirit up,
Sustain your heart, and nerve your arm.

Take up your cross, nor heed the shame,
Nor let your foolish heart rebel;
For you the Lord endured the cross
To save your soul from death and hell.

Take up your cross and follow Christ,
Nor think till death to lay it down;
For only those who bear the cross
May hope to wear a golden crown.

Irving Lowens comments on the tune KEDRON in *Music and Musicians in Early America,* where he points out that few folk hymns appeared in print in the eighteenth century:

A few authentic folk hymns can be found in the tune-books of the late 1790s. See for example, Amos Pilsbury's *The United States' Sacred Harmony* (Boston, 1799), which contains (among others) the first known printing of KEDRON, one of the loveliest and most popular of all folk hymns. It is interesting to note that Pilsbury himself was a Southerner active in Charleston, South Carolina.[2]

In true folk-tune tradition, KEDRON appears in varied forms. Following is KEDRON as it appeared in the tenor voice in four important early nineteenth-century tune books:

Table 1

Repository of Sacred Music, Part Second, John Wyeth, 1813, p. 43.

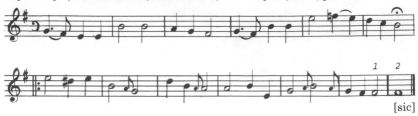

[sic]

Kentucky Harmony, Ananias Davisson, 1816, p. 14.

Genuine Church Music (later, *Harmonia Sacra*), Joseph Funk, 1832, p. 165.

Southern Harmony, William Walker, 1835, p. 3.

All the books used the time signature , and each editor explained its meaning. Wyeth, for example, gives this table under "Moods of Common Time" in his introduction (p. 13):

The first mood is known by a plain C and has a Semibreve [○] or its quantity in a measure, sung in the time of four seconds, four beats in a bar, two down and two up.

The second mood is known by a C with a stroke thro it, has the same measure, sung in the time of three seconds, four beats in a bar, two down and two up. [He forgot to add the stroke.]

The third mood is known by C inverted, sometimes with a stroke thro it, has the same measure sung in the time of two seconds, has two beats in a bar, one down and the other up.

The fourth mood is known by figure 2 over a figure 3 [sic], has a Minim [♩] for its measure note, sung in the time of one second, two beats in a bar, one down and the other up.

KEDRON is in the third mood.

Wyeth's concern for conveying tempo accurately as early as 1813 is impressive. The metronome, with its mechanical means of measuring speed, did not appear until 1816 in Europe. Previously, tempo might be indicated by human motions, such as the pulse rate of a quietly breathing man.

Modern hymnals (See the Episcopal, Methodist, Harvard, and Yale, as well as *MH*) rearrange KEDRON to adjust it to the natural triple groupings—either as ♪♩♩♩♩♩♩ or ♪♩♩♩♩♩♩♩ . There were many instances similar to KEDRON in which nineteenth-century editors grouped triple folk tunes in duple notation, thus creating an interesting cross rhythm. One could theorize that the bar lines did not signify a strong beat in those days, but evidence negates that possibility. The *Easy Instructor,* 1798 (see below p. 90), had a footnote to a description of time: "The hand falls at the beginning of every bar in all moods of time" (p. 11). And Joseph Funk said that in beating time—which "should be performed with decency and order, and without the least sign of ostentation"—that the hand should fall on the first part of every measure in all moods of time.[3]

Present hymnals have adopted the *Southern Harmony* form of KEDRON (Table 1, number 4), except for its duple organization. The compilers of *The Mennonite Hymnal,* however, used Funk's version (Fig. 13) because of its strong influence on Virginia and Pennsylvania Mennonites to the present day. At the asterisk (*) his version (Table 1, number 3) is strikingly different from the other three; ** has one change of note. The insertion of D# at *** is even stranger. The interval from D# to C is hard to sing. Perhaps Funk, like some of the northern tune-book editors, preferred to modernize the natural minor mode of the folk tunes by changing it to harmonic minor with a D#. Lowens suggests that Funk may not have approved totally of the folk idiom.[4] Funk's version differs from the others in its metrical arrangement also. The first half begins with an upbeat of one-half measure.

Figure 13

Genuine Church Music
Joseph Funk.
Winchester: J. W. Hollis, Printer (Published at the Office of the Republican), 1832.
p. 165.

All of the editions made use of the four shapes (see p. 82). Apparently some of the European-educated musicians of New England—Mason and Hastings especially—were embarrassed by the crudeness of the shape notes and introduced a *do, re, mi* system in its place. Funk defended the shapes in a lengthy section called, "Remarks on the Use of Patent [shape]

Notes," which he said were sometimes called *character* notes. This is a small part of his argument.

Now, I would ask those who exclaim so loudly, and I may say, so unreasonably, against the using of the patent notes—Do they, in any wise, retard the progress of the diligent and inquisitive student? The strongest objections which I have yet met with, from the most inveterate enemies to the patent notes, are the following: 1. "That people can learn to sing so easily, that they will not learn well." 2. "That the patent notes have always been found to curb inquiry after musical knowledge, by satisfying the student with the shadow, to the entire loss of the substance." 3. "That notes are *representatives* of musical *sounds,* and if so, how can a knowledge of their *names* qualify a person to understand their sounds?" . . . On the first and second objections (both of which are of one meaning), I would make the following remarks. I have been a teacher of vocal music for many years, both in the English and German languages, in which time I taught both by round and patent notes; and I believe there was more *inquiry* made concerning the rudiments of music by my patent-note singers than by those who sung the round notes. Now I think the reason for this is plain, inasmuch as the patent-note singers have more time to make *inquiry* than the singers of round notes have; for it is evident, that much of the time of the round-note singers must be taken up in finding by calculation the names of their notes, whereas the patent-note singers have the names communicated to their minds on sight. [5]

Solmization, or the use of syllables for sight-reading music, was a practice which went back to the early eleventh century. At that time an Italian monk, Guido d'Arezzo, devised a system of syllable names for successive tones of the scale from the hymn to John the Baptist. [6]

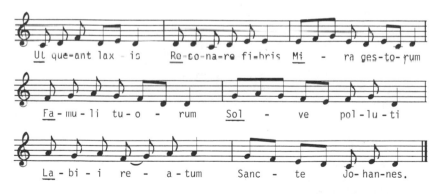

These syllables *ut, re, mi, fa, sol,* and *la,* continued to be useful through the following centuries.

The first American music textbook, by John Tufts, 1721, recommended the *fa sol la* method, placing the first letter of each syllable directly on a staff, instead of notes. The beginning of OLD HUNDREDTH, for example, looked like this:

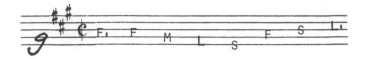

The system was superior to the British Tonic-Sol-Fa approach because Tufts placed the letters high and low on a staff.

It was an imaginative idea to move from a letter to notes with varied shapes of heads. The four shapes of the early folk-tune books came from *The Easy Instructor,* "deposited for copyright June 15, 1798." The names William Little and William Smith appear on the title page of many of the editions. [7]

Here is OLD HUNDREDTH in the four shapes for *mi, fa, sol,* and *la*:

In 1846 Jesse B. Aikin published his *Christian Minstrel* in Philadelphia with seven shapes. He added *do* △, *re* ▽, and *si (ti)* ◖ to the *Easy Instructor* shapes. By 1851 Joseph Funk and his sons expanded their shapes to seven also: *do* ◻, *re* ◁, and *ti* ▷. With this fifth edition of *Genuine Church Music* he changed the name of his compilation to *Harmonia Sacra.* [8] The book has retained its unique shape notes through the twenty-third edition, 1972. Aikin's seven-character notes came into Mennonite use in *Hymns and Tunes,* 1890, and they continue in the shape-note edition of *The Mennonite Hymnal.*

Genuine Church Music, 1832, is a valuable historical document for Mennonites for a number of reasons. First, it indicates that early in the change from German to English, Mennonites were concerned for "good" music. Funk said in his preface:

While I submit the following compilation to the taste of competent judges, I entertain the hope that they will, on due examination, discover it to be a good book of its kind. A large portion of the compositions here brought together, copied from what I believe to be their best forms, consists of those dignified, solemn, and heart-affecting productions of musical genius which have stood the test of time, and survived the changes of fashion. Such music will never become obsolete in the house of God; it cannot even lose a particle of its interest, while human nature remains unaltered. No frequency of use can wear out these venerable airs; no fondness of novelty can make us insensible to their sterling merit. (p. iv)

The fact that he had in his library the first edition, 1822, of *The Boston Handel and Haydn Society Collection of Church Music,* edited by Lowell Mason, and *Musica Sacra* of Hastings and Warriner, 1829 edition, suggests that he preferred the European styles the New Englanders advocated. But he had also Freeman Lewis's *The Beauties of Harmony,* which included folk materials. [9]

Second, Funk was interested in music education. George Pullen Jackson says of Funk's preface—"the best written, most dignified, cogent, and concise one in any of the southern books." [10] He had thought through various methods of learning, as we saw in his defense of shape notes; he explained carefully how to read the moods of time, keys, and their transpositions, accents, and emphasis; how to beat time and how to understand poetic meters. As was the custom with tune books, he included "practical lessons for tuning the voice." This and a few similar books were the texts for singing schools that thrived among Mennonites until the middle of the twentieth century. Attending the annual *Harmonia Sacra* singing at Weavers Mennonite Church near Harrisonburg, Virginia, on January 1, 1964, I was astonished at the crowd's ability to sing anything from the book.

Third, *Genuine Church Music* provided the tunes for the first American Mennonite hymnbook in English, *A Selection of Psalms, Hymns and Spiritual Songs . . .,* 1847. No tunes are included in that book, but in each case a tune name is given. The preface indicates that "the names of the tunes at the beginning of each hymn correspond with the Music Book entitled 'Harmonia Sacra.' "

[1] Minneapolis: Augsburg Publishing House, p. 8.

[2] New York: Norton, 1964, p. 139.

[3] I still remember from my childhood the strange effect of singing J. S. Shoemaker's hymn, "We all have met to worship thee, And glorify thy name, dear Lord." The music was naturally triple but it was barred in duple. This and two other songs (numbers 11 and 88) written by the committee of *Hymns and Tunes,* 1890, still retained this curious folk characteristic.

[4] In speaking of Wyeth, Lowens says, "Funk borrowed 11 [tunes] for his *Geniune Church Music,* despite his professed abhorrence for such 'ephemera.' " I count at least 16; Lowens omitted KEDRON and 4 others in his tabulations (pp. viii-ix). John Wyeth, *Repository of Sacred Music, Part Second,* p. x.

[5]Joseph Funk, *Genuine Church Music,* p. xx.

[6]*Liber Usualis.* Tournai: Desclee Company, 1962, p. 1504.

[7]For the history of this important tune book see Lowen's *Music and Musicians,* chapter 6, p. 115.

[8]The 12th edition, 1867, rearranged in the shape-note edition of *The Mennonite Hymnal.*

[9]See Grace I. Showalter, "The Library and Manuscripts of Joseph Funk," in *EMC Bulletin,* January 1967, pp. 11-12.

[10]*White Spirituals,* p. 47.

147. My Dear Redeemer and My Lord. SOCIAL BAND.

The text, "My Dear Redeemer," comes from Isaac Watts's *Hymns and Spiritual Songs,* 1707-09, Book II, "Songs Composed on Divine Subjects." The four-stanza hymn is subtitled "The Example of Christ."

General Conference Mennonites, with the 1894 book, had sung the text to HAMBURG, which frequently is linked with "When I Survey the Wondrous Cross" (*MH* 167). The words joined with ROCKINGHAM NEW (*MH* 398) in the 1927 *Mennonite Hymn Book.* The *Mennonite Hymnary,* 1940, dropped the hymn. The Mennonite Church had sung "My Dear Redeemer" to MISSIONARY CHANT in the *Church Hymnal.* Beginning on a complex upbeat was difficult for song leaders in the unaccompanied tradition, and phrase endings often sounded awkward. Therefore, we looked for a folk tune from *Harmonia Sacra* (later editions of Funk's *Genuine Church Music*). Although the text is long meter, we chose a tune in long meter double—SOCIAL BAND. Thus the four stanzas are reduced to two.

The tune first appeared in Jeremiah Ingalls's collection called *Christian Harmony; or Songster's Companion,* published in New Hampshire in 1805. Ingalls, a Vermont farmer and cooper, was one of the first compilers to incorporate folk tunes and camp-meetings songs in a tune book. Gilbert Chase described the book as containing a number of lively tunes, obviously taken from secular sources, which sounded to him reminiscent of English, Scottish, and Irish popular tunes. [1]

SOCIAL BAND, which is called SHOUTING HYMN in Ingalls's book, must have been used at camp meetings. The first two of its twenty-one, long-meter stanzas are needed to sing through the tune once. The first two stanzas are reproduced in Figure 14.

Shouting Hymn.

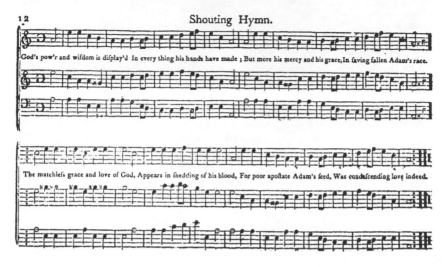

God's pow'r and wifdom is difplay'd In every thing his hands have made ; But more his mercy and his grace, In faving fallen Adam's race.

The matchlefs grace and love of God, Appears in fhedding of his blood, For poor apoftate Adam's feed, Was condefcending love indeed.

Figure 14

Microfilm from the Newberry Library, 60 West Walton Street, Chicago, Illinois 60610

Christian Harmony.
Jeremiah Ingalls.
Exeter; N.H., 1805.

The poem proceeds in ballad fashion, telling the story of Jesus coming to earth and dying for sinners. Stanza 4 says:
    That God who heav'n and earth did frame,
    Who counts the stars and calls their name,
    He, for our sakes did stoop so far
    As to become a carpenter.
In stanza 8 the narrator enters:
    Methinks I heard his father say,
    "The utmost farthing you shall pay;
    My injured justice must have right,
    I can't abate one single mite. . . ."
After the vivid story of Christ's death, stanza 20 says:
    Arise, ye stupid souls and view
    What your dear Lord has done for you;
    And spend the remnant of your days
    In striving to advance his praise.
A doxology closes the hymn.[2]
    At some time in the few decades following 1805 a new text came with the tune SHOUTING HYMN. Funk included it in the second edition of

Genuine Church Music, 1835, calling it SOCIAL BAND and giving "Dover Selec." as its source. The first two long meter stanzas were:

Say now ye lovely social band,
Who walk the way to Canaan's land;
Ye who have fled from Sodom's plain
Say, do you wish to turn again?
Have you just ventured to the field,
Well armed with helmet, sword and shield;
And shall the world with dread alarms
Compel you now to ground your arms. [3]

As was the case with KEDRON, the tune appeared in various forms—even with various names—from one tune book to another.

The northerner, Ingalls, used sharps to make harmonic minor. The other versions are in natural minor, common to many folk tunes. Rhythms vary also.

One other folk tune comes from Jeremiah Ingalls's book—VERNON (*MH* 322), though Ingalls called it WISDOM. The middle of three voices had the melody (as was usual for Ingalls):

Wyeth's *Repository . . . Part Second,* 1813, labeled the tune VERNON and linked it with Charles Wesley's "Come, O Thou Traveller Unknown." Wyeth attributed the melody to Chapin, a New Englander. (The *Original Sacred Harp* (1911) editor seems to have misread the name and has inserted F. F. Chopin for both VERNON and CLAMANDA!) Possibly Funk borrowed the text and tune combination from Wyeth, and the compilers of *The Mennonite Hymnal* are indebted to Funk.[4]

"Come, O Thou Traveller" is a fine ballad-like narrative based on the story of Jacob's wrestling with the angel. We included only four stanzas of the original fourteen, published in Charles Wesley's *Hymns and Sacred Poems,* 1742. Wesley is the focus of the next essay.

[1] *America's Music.* New York: McGraw-Hill, 1955, pp. 137-38.

[2] Reading this "Shouting Hymn" brings memories of another ballad, "Saw Ye My Savior," deeply entrenched in Mennonite Church tradition until *The Mennonite Hymnal,* 1969, omitted it:

Saw ye my Savior, saw ye my Savior,
Saw ye my Savior and God?
Oh! he died on Calvary to atone for you and me
And to purchase our pardon with blood.

The poem had eight verses in all:

2 He was extended . . .
3 Jesus hung bleeding . . .
4 Darkness prevailed . . .

The *Church Hymnal* stopped there, with verse 4 ending:

Oh, the solid rocks were rent, thro' creation's vast extent
When the Jews crucified the Lord.

The triumphant conclusion and promise of forgiveness were omitted. The hymn always appeared at Communion in my congregation, and emerged unannounced, with the bishop leading.

[3] Funk, 1972 edition, p. 268.

[4] The C-sharp is a foreign intrusion in the soprano near the end. Otherwise it is a natural-minor version. We do not remember why we inserted it! Choirs could learn the tune omitting the sharp.

100. Ye Servants of God. HANOVER.

Julian's *Dictionary of Hymnology* presents five members of the remarkable Wesley family—Samuel, the father, and four of his hymn-writing children—Samuel, John, Charles, and Mehetabel. The section on Charles begins:

But, after all, it was Charles Wesley who was the *great* hymn-writer of the Wesley family,—perhaps taking quantity and quality into consideration, the greatest hymn-writer of all ages. (p. 1257)

Charles Wesley was certainly remarkable in the quantity of hymns he wrote. Frank Baker in *Representative Verse of Charles Wesley* (London: Epworth Press, 1962) has counted nearly nine thousand extant hymns, thirteen hundred still in manuscript, in comparison to about one thousand by Isaac Watts one generation earlier. Baker counted lines as well, and estimated that Wesley needed to average ten lines of poetry every day for fifty years in order to produce his hymns, and to complete an extant poem every other day. (p. xi)

The quality of his hymns is revealed through a number of aspects of his poetic style. (1) He handled meter with imagination. Watts, his predecessor, wrote almost entirely in the three psalm meters (L.M., C.M., S.M.). Among the twenty-four Wesley texts in *The Mennonite Hymnal* there are fourteen different meters. (2) Most of Watts's were iambic in accent (rising from unaccented to accented), but Wesley built on iambic, trochaic (falling), anapaestic (two rising syllables to an accent), and occasional mixtures. (3) His rhyme schemes lend coherence, even though they usually affect us subconsciously. Watts often settled for only two rhyming lines out of four lines. Wesley usually had a much tighter structure, incorporating every final syllable of the line in his scheme— consecutive rhyming—*a a b b*, cross rhyming—*a b a b*, or more complicated plans. Occasionally he used the unusual double rhyme (see pp. 105-106), consisting of a heavy-light ending, which is called a *feminine* ending.

Listed below are selected hymns of Wesley which illustra te the variety of his poetic resources:[1]

MH	Hymn (&Choice of St.)	St.	Meter	Accent	Rhyme Scheme
350	A Charge to Keep I Have (ALL)	2	S.M.D. (6.6.8.6.6.6.8.6.)	iambic	*a b a b c d c d*
330	Soldiers of Christ Arise (1a,1b,2a,2b,16a,16b)	16	S.M.D.	mixed: iamb & trochaic	*a b a b c d c d*
104	O For a Thousand Tongues (7,8,9,10,1)	18	C.M. (8.6.8.6.)	iambic	*a b a b*
430	Forth in Thy Name (1,2,4,6)	6	L.M. (8.8.8.8.)	iambic	*a b a b*
184	Rejoice, The Lord Is King (1,2,3,4)	6	6.6.6.6.8.8.	iambic	*a b a b c c*
272	O How Happy Are They (1,2,3,4)	7	5.5.9.5.5.9. (alt. 6.6.9.6.6.9.)	anapaestic	*a a b c c b*
236	Jesus, Lover of My Soul (1,2,4,5)	5	7.7.7.7.7.7.7.7.	trochaic	*a b a b c d c d*
75	Love Divine, All Loves Excelling (ALL)	4	8.7.8.7.8.7.8.7.	trochaic	*a b a b c d c d* Feminine endings
322	Come, O Thou Traveller Unknown (1,4,9,10)	14	8.8.8.8.8.8.	iambic	*a b a b c c*

Bernard L. Manning, who wrote a lively and engaging book, *The Hymns of Wesley and Watts*, commented as follows on the pauses in Wesley's poetry:

> More than most writers, Wesley makes the end of his lines correspond with natural pauses in his thought. The sound and the sense coincide. This is it which makes his verse specially suitable for singing. This is it which makes it possible to sing his hymns so easily to the so-called "old-fashioned" tunes, the florid, repetitious tunes, in which any line may be repeated almost at random in almost accidental combinations. [2]

Baker, on the same subject, says:

> The very *size* of his stanzas was conditioned by his logical approach. He wanted a stanza in which a theme could be announced, developed, and satisfactorily concluded—with a foreshadowing of the theme for the following stanza. . . . Within the stanzas themselves we find an orderly synchronization of thought and verse. In general, every line contains a complete idea, is in fact a clause or a sentence. Similarly every stanza is a paragraph, and the whole poem a logically constructed essay in verse. [3]

The logic is so attractive that the omission of stanzas often is a great pity. To read the whole of "Come, O Thou Traveller Unknown" (*MH* 322), for example, is far better than the four verses we have. In that poem the existence of both unity and variation in the last lines of the fourteen stanzas contribute much to the progression. By way of contrast, the use of only a fragment of a poem such as "The Sands of Time Are Sinking" (see pp. 43-46), seems more acceptable.

Both Baker [4] and Manning [5] speak of the richness Wesley achieved by the judicious use of Latin-derived words (often polysyllabic) in his Anglo-Saxon texture. He was a scholar of the classics and handled language with felicity. Baker described Wesley's skill in using adjectives and adverbs ending in *able, ably, ible, ibly*, without disturbing the flow. Further examples of Latinate words are:

MH 322   St. 2 unutterable St. 3 universal St. 4 unspeakable
MH 244   St. 2 intercede St. 3 effectual
MH 115   St. 1 long-expected; consolation St. 2 sufficient
MH 432   St. 3 inmost substance St. 4 delightfully

"Ye Servants of God" (*MH* 100), was written "To be Sung in a Tumult." Around the time of the Jacobite Rebellion of 1745 Methodists were identified as Jacobites and falsely accused as leaders of rebellion against the king. The persecutions of Methodists stimulated the publication of thirty-three songs in a booklet called *Hymns for Times of Trouble and Persecution,* 1744. The second and third omitted stanzas contain more suggestions of tumult than do the stanzas in *The Mennonite Hymnal* (1, 4, 5, and 6 of the original).

2 The Waves of the Sea Have lifted up their Voice,
   Sore troubled that we In Jesus rejoice;
   The Floods they are roaring, But Jesus is here,
   While we are adoring, He always is near.

3 Men, Devils engage, The Billows arise,
   And horribly rage, And threaten the Skies:
   Their Fury shall never Our Stedfastness shock,
   The weakest Believer Is built on a Rock.[6]

The meter 10.10.11.11. breaks down into 5s and 6s: 5.5.5.5.6.5.5.6.5., with pauses in the long line which follow the thought skillfully. The rhyme scheme is *a a b b*, but the half-lines rhyme as well, creating an *a b a b c d c d* pattern for a stanza. The poetic meter is anapaestic, consisting of ᴗ ᴗ — (light, light, heavy).

The triple time of HANOVER suits the anapaestic meter well. In addition, the shape of the melody supports the pauses in the poetry. The first and fourth long phrases end with a hemiola effect (see pp. 107-108) The end of the fourth, for example is:

The use of this tune is probably still troublesome to those who have known LYONS (*MH* 15) but not HANOVER. The first phrase is confusing unless the keyboard first presents at least the initial long phrase or the song leader sings it alone.

William Croft (1678-1727) probably composed HANOVER (as well as ST. ANNE, *MH* 84). It appeared first in Tate and Brady's *Supplement to the New Version,* 1708 (see p. 55), for Psalm 67. Handel, who came to England from Hanover, Germany, soon after the tune was published, was credited with its composition; thus the name.

---

[1] With assistance from Baker, pp. 396-403, "Charles Wesley's Metres: Notes and Index."

[2] Bernard L. Manning, *The Hymns of Wesley and Watts.* London: Epworth Press, 1942, p. 59.

[3] Baker, p. xxxvi.

[4] *Ibid.,* pp. xviii-xix.

[5] Manning, 24 fl.

[6] Baker, p. 50.

244. Arise, My Soul, Arise. LENOX.

"Arise, My Soul, Arise" (*MH* 244), was published in *Hymns and Sacred Poems,* 1742, in five stanzas of six lines each, titled "Behold the Man!" Stanza 4, omitted in *The Mennonite Hymnal* reads:

The Father hears Him pray,
  His dear Anointed One,
He cannot turn away
  The Presence of His Son:
His Spirit answers to the Blood,
And tells me, I am born of God.[1]

The meter, 6.6.6.6.8.8., is matched by the rhyme scheme, *a b a b c c,* which sets off and emphasizes the last two lines of each stanza.

"Ye Servants of God" is an exuberant congregational expression. In "Arise, My Soul, Arise" Wesley turns inward and considers his most basic theme: God and the soul. "He is always at Calvary; no other place in the universe matters."[2] Watts takes a sweeping look at the universe—"Ere the blue heav'ns were stretched abroad," "Were the whole realm of nature mine"—but Wesley focuses on his experience with Christ. Manning says again:

Why do Wesley's hymns confirm and restore our confidence, and build us up securely in our most holy faith? It is no doubt partly because they show us something of the life of one of the pure in heart who saw God. We may not see God. We cannot fail to see that Wesley saw him. Purity of heart: we are near Wesley's secret there; scriptural holiness, purity of heart, inevitably reflected in his clear mind and limpid verse. . . . He is obsessed with the greatest things, and he confirms our faith because he shows us these above all the immediate, local, fashionable problems and objections to the faith. We move to the serener air. We sit in heavenly places with Christ Jesus.[3]

LENOX was originally an early American fuging-tune. It is not at all an attempt to imitate the European fugue, but its roots go back to the English fuging psalm-tunes and Scottish psalms "in Reports"—tunes that incorporate imitative techniques.[4] English fuging-tunes were published first in America in James Lyon's *Urania,* 1761.[5]

LENOX, by Lewis Edson, Sr. (1748-1820)[6] published first in Simeon Jocelyn's *The Chorister's Companion,* 1782 or 1783, gives us a classic example of the American fuging-tune. The melody is in the tenor. The following version was copied from Isaiah Thomas's *Worcester Collection of Sacred Harmony,* 1786,[7] although the first half of the piece was laid out in four staves rather than two. The first phrases (6.6.6.6.) are in block style, with words sung simultaneously in all parts. Then the fuging begins (on 8.8.). The bass leads and following voices enter one at a time, one measure apart.

Ye tribes of Ad - am. *[sic]* join with heav'n and earth and seas;

And of - fer notes di - vine To your Cre - a - tor's praise.

Ye ho-ly throng of an-gels bright, In

Ye ho-ly throng of

Ye ho-ly throng of an-gels bright, Ye ho-ly throng of

Ye ho-ly throng of an-gels bright, Ye ho-ly throng of an-gels bright, In

worlds of light, Be - gin the song. song.

an-gels bright, In worlds of light, Be - gin the song. song.

an-gels bright, In worlds of light, Be - gin the song. song.

worlds of light, Be - gin the song. song.

George Pullen Jackson points out that fuging-tunes are found in all the southern books except *Genuine Church Music*. He comments further:

Father [sic] Joseph Funk had no "fondness for novelty" and "the changes of fashion" in sacred music. His GCM, therefore, contained not one fuging [his spelling links it with the European fugue] piece. Ananias Davisson must have had such people as his neighbor in mind when he wrote (*Kentucky Harmony,* p. 14): "There are some of our superannuated old *Deacons,* who stand in opposition to fuging [sic] music; but it is an old maxim, and I think a very just one too, *that variety is always pleasing."* Hence, we find many fuging pieces in the popular *Kentucky Harmony* and its *Supplement.* All the Tennessee, South Carolina, and Georgia books, and the *Missouri Harmony,* have from twenty to seventy songs each, built on the fuging plan, the number depending somewhat on the size of the book.[8]

Funk rearranged LENOX. The fuging part looks like this:

(Text: "Hark! the Notes of Joy" still used in <u>Harmonia Sacra</u>.)   *etc.*

Jackson was right. Funk adopted no fuging-tunes for his 1832 edition. Occasionally a voice drops out for variety, as in the above example, but Funk rearranged all imitative passages. And *MH* 244 removes even Funk's variety; all four parts sing all of the time. In light of the interest Mennonites in the 1970s have taken in three Early American imitative pieces—*MH* 74, 606, and 613—we should have reinstated the fuging section of LENOX. Choirs could try it.

Mennonites must have borrowed the text-tune combination (for *Church and Sunday School Hymnal,* 1902) from the Methodists, who brought the two together at least by 1878 in *Hymns of the Methodist Episcopal Church.*

[1] Baker, p. 45.
[2] Manning, p. 43.
[3] *Ibid.,* p. 47.

[4] See Chapter 14, "The Origins of the American Fuging-Tune," in *Music and Musicians* . . . by I. Lowens for a full account of this genre.

[5] See an *original* copy of *Urania* in the J. D. Hartzler Collection at Goshen College. Hartzler, an Iowa Mennonite farmer, has spent his lifetime gathering a valuable collection (2,745 volumes) of eighteenth- and nineteenth-century American hymnals and tune books.

[6] Lowens's chapter 9 in *Music and Musicians* . . . is "The Musical Edsons of Shady: Early American Tunesmiths," pp. 178-93.

[7] I checked it also with Oliver Holden's *The Union Harmony,* vol. 1, 1793. His tune CORONATION is at *MH* 95.

[8] *White Spirituals in the Southern Uplands.* New York: Dover Reprint, 1965, pp. 207-9.

38. All Glory Be to God on High.
ALLEIN GOTT IN DER HÖH.

Martin Luther (1483-1546) broke with the Roman Catholic Church in the years immediately following 1517, when he posted his ninety-five theses on the church door at Wittenberg. His views on worship and music have influenced Protestants deeply ever since.

Luther's insistence on the full participation of the congregation in worship led to the emergence of two kinds of music, both with vernacular texts. The first was a German liturgical music comparable to that of the Latin Mass and Offices, and the second was a new kind of hymn, the *choral* (English, chorale) or *Kirchenlied*. "All Glory Be to God on High," *MH* 38, which is based on the Latin *Gloria in Excelsis Deo,* serves as a point of reference for both types.

Luther concerned himself in the early 1520s with revising the liturgy. The sixteenth-century Anabaptists were radical reformers who were willing to abolish the Roman liturgy. Luther, however, valued the forms he had inherited, and in a pamphlet, *Concerning the Order of Public Worship,* 1523, he set forth a plan and rationale for a Communion service:

> We therefore assert: It is not now nor ever has been our intention to abolish the liturgical service of God completely, but rather to purify the one that is now in use from the wretched accretions which corrupt it and to point out an evangelical use. [1]

He mentioned the sung parts of the Ordinary of the Mass—*Kyrie eleison, Gloria in Excelsis Deo, Credo, Sanctus,* and *Agnus Dei,* whose texts are always the same—as well as the Propers, whose texts change with the season.

> We accept the *Kyrie eleison* in the form in which it has been used until now, with the various melodies for different seasons, together with the

Angelic Hymn, *Gloria in Excelsis,* which follows it. However, the bishop may decide to omit the latter as often as he wishes. [2]

The *Gloria in Excelsis* is the "Angelic Hymn" because it begins with the song of the angels recorded in Luke 2:14, "Glory to God in the highest, and on earth peace, good will towards men."

The English prose translation of the entire *Gloria* from the *Book of Common Prayer,* 1550, appears at *MH* 632. The date, "Before 500 A.D." at *MH* 632 is probably appropriate. Exact dates for ancient texts are, of course, difficult. Gregory Dix in *The Shape of the Liturgy* reports that Pope Symmachus (A.D. 498-514) "Ordained that on every Sunday and martyr's feast the hymn 'Glory be to God on high' should be said." He comments further:

> The *Gloria* was no new composition when it was put to this new use at Rome *c.* A.D. 500. It is found in Egypt, Syria and Asia Minor in the fourth-fifth century, and is said to have been introduced into the West by S. Hilary of Poitiers *c.* A.D. 363, who had come upon it during his banishment in the East. The number of local variants in the text of the hymn already found in the fourth century indicate an origin in the third, or even perhaps the second century. [3]

The *Gloria* in German, probably by Luther himself, was published by 1537. Each phrase is eight syllables long, and phrases group in rhyming pairs for antiphonal singing. These are the first three of seventeen pairs:

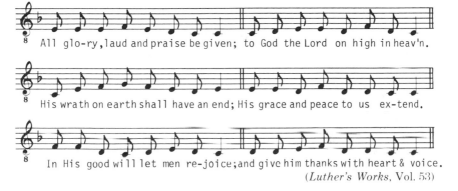

(*Luther's Works,* Vol. 53)

MH 38 is a chorale version of the *Gloria in Excelsis.* (See pp. 50-51 for previous comments on chorales.) It is strophic, meaning that all four of its verses use the same music. Luther Noss, in *Christian Hymns,* claimed that "the text was prepared in 1522 by Nikolaus Decius, a Benedictine monk who had recently joined the Reformation movement. It is the earliest example of its kind in the German evangelical tradition, preceding Martin Luther's first hymn by at least a year. The text was first published in 1525, without music." [4] Its language was Low German. The High German version, which is given at *MH* 38, was published in Valten

Schumann's *Gesang Buch,* 1539, with the proper tune, ALLEIN GOTT IN DER HÖH.

The melody for ALLEIN GOTT is derived from the musical setting of the *Gloria* for the Easter season. Handbooks differ in their information on the date and arranger of the first appearance. Many of them give Thomas Müntzer, 1524; others, Schumann, 1539. Johann Kulp, however, asserts that Nikolaus Decius arranged the music, and that both text and music existed without a doubt in 1522 in Braunschweig.[5] The radical reformer, Müntzer, made a German version in his *Deutsche Evangelische Messe* in 1524, which is at least a very early source for the 1539 tune. Here are the Latin and Müntzer versions along with the first two phrases of the 1539 melody:[6]

Early chorale melodies were often derived from a previous work—from a chant, as in the case of ALLEIN GOTT, or a secular song, such as INNSBRUCK (see pp. 53-54). Many of the tunes were, like ALLEIN GOTT, in German *Bar* form, consisting of two *Stollen* and an *Abgesang,* thus making an *a a b* form. (The fragment copied is the first of the *Stollen.*) *Bar* form was a common organization of German medieval songs of the *Minnesinger* and of the *Meistersinger,* their successors. The mastersingers were still thriving in the sixteenth century, and the rearrangement of through-composed (i.e., no section repeats; stanzas have new music) chant into a *Bar*-form composition was a clear connection with secular and popular sources.

Nine out of the sixteen German tunes in *The Mennonite Hymnal* written within the first fifty years of the Lutheran movement (1524-74) are in *Bar* form. They are, in addition to ALLEIN GOTT:

MH	TUNE NAME	DATE	ZAHN NO.
611	CHRIST LAG IN TODESBANDEN	1524	7012a
234	AUS TIEFER NOT	1525	4438a
325 597	EIN FESTE BURG	1529	7377a
384	NUN FREUT EUCH	1535	4429a
40	NUN WEND IHR HÖREN	1540	Bäumker No. 26
173	O LAMM GOTTES	1542	4360
178	AVE VIRGO VIRGINUM	1544	6285
21 247	MIT FREUDEN ZART	1566	8186

Bar form, *a a b,* has its own peculiar psychological impact on us. It makes a statement which it repeats and reinforces before departing to the contrasting *b.* It does not return to the familiar *a,* as *a b a* hymns would do. (See pp. 23-24.) In the early history of western music *a a b* was a more basic form than *a b a.* It was used in French and Italian secular songs of the eleventh to fourteenth centuries, as well as in *Minnesinger* and *Meistersinger* songs.

The German text of *MH* 38 was translated by Catherine Winkworth (1827-78). She published four books of translations within fourteen years—*Lyra Germanica,* Series 1, 1855 and 2, 1858, *Chorale-Book for England* (with the proper tunes also), 1863, and *Christian Singers of Germany,* 1869. The last of these is a series of biographies of hymn writers, with an engraving of Hans Sachs (d. 1576), the most famous of *Meistersinger,* placed appropriately on the title page.

In 1892 Julian's *Dictionary of Hymnology* said that her translations from German "are the most widely used of any from that language, and have had more to do with the modern revival of the English use of German hymns than the versions of any other writer."[7]

Winkworth's concern for the craft of translating is revealed in her preface to the *Chorale-Book for England,* 1863, where she wrote:

As a rule, the hymn and tune have been considered as one and indivisible, and the original metres therefore strictly preserved for the sake of the tunes, which would not admit of any deviation without detriment to their characteristic beauty. This has necessitated the frequent use of the double rhymes, which the structure of the German language renders as common, and indeed inevitable, in German, as monosyllabic rhymes are with us. The comparatively small number of the former in our language presents a serious obstacle to rendering the German hymns into English with the force and simplicity they possess in their own tongue, and without which they cannot become truly naturalized among us; yet it is one which must be encountered if the tunes also are to be introduced with them, as they ought to be, and in their proper form.[8]

MH 38 has double rhyme at the ends of the *a* sections: *-friended* and *ended; ever* and *never; Father* and *gather; -failing* and *-vailing.* Double rhymes come at the ends of phrases in which the next-to-the-last syllable is stressed; the last is light.

The Mennonite Hymnal has thirty Winkworth translations from German, in contrast to five by A. T. Russell and three by Robert Bridges, Frances E. Cox, and Richard Massie. A few poets like John Wesley are represented by two translations and many authors by one. Thus Catherine Winkworth's work stands out significantly above all others.

One hundred years after the *Chorale-Book for England* Erik Routley commented on its significance:

The *Chorale-Book for England,* then, ranks with the work of Neale [p. 19] and Helmore as an historic gesture towards the broadening of the English hymn-singer's vocabulary. It stands thus directly in the tradition of the Wesleys, who alone attempted anything like it before that group of which Miss Winkworth was the most distinguished member. Her successors were Bridges [pp. 51-53] and Woodward, both of whom a generation later sought the same end—to make fine historic music of another culture available to Englishmen by writing hymns that would carry it. The *Chorale-Book* is unique only in this—that the material contained in it maintains a higher level of translator's faithfulness, and achieves a far higher combined index of fidelity, quantity, literary grace, and congregational acceptability than any work of its kind attempted before—or since.[9]

[1] "An Order of Mass and Communion" in *Luther's Works,* vol. 53, *Liturgy and Hymns.* Philadelphia: Fortress Press, 1965, p. 20. Translated by P. Z. Stodach and U. S. Leupold.

[2] *Ibid.,* p. 23.

[3] Westminster: Dacre Press, 1945, p. 456.

[4] Cleveland: World Publishing Co., 1963, no. 5.

[5] *Handbuch zum Evangelischen Kirchengesangbuch.* Göttingen: Vandenboeck and Ruprecht, 1958, p. 209.

[6] Latin from *Liber Usualis,* pp. 16-17; Müntzer from Paul Kirn and Günther Franz, *Thomas Müntzer: Schriften und Briefe.* Gütersloh: Gütersloher Verlagshaus Gerd Mohn, 1968, p. 193; ALLEIN GOTT; Zahn no. 4457.

[7] Julian, p. 1287.

[8] London: Longman, Green, Longman, Roberts, and Green, 1865 ed., p. vi.

[9] *The Hymn Society of Great Britain and Ireland Bulletin,* no 99, p. 186.

20. Praise Thou the Lord, O My Soul.
LOBE DEN HERREN, O MEINE SEELE.

LOBE DEN HERREN, O MEINE SEELE, *MH* 20 (not to be confused with LOBE DEN HERREN, DEN MÄCHTIGEN KÖNIG, *MH* 9) is an anonymous seventeenth-century tune in *Bar* form *a a b* and in triple time. Although *Bar* form had been a dominant pattern for sixteenth-century chorales since Luther's day, triple time was not usual. But by the end of the sixteenth century, triple chorales were appearing with greater frequency.

ALLEIN GOTT, *MH* 38, and MIT FREUDEN ZART, *MH* 21, 247, are the two clear triple-meter tunes of the first fifty years of chorales. In the period 1574 to 1700 many triple tunes emerged, and a number of them are the most popular chorales still in use. For example, IN DIR IST FREUDE, 1591 (*MH* 90), is a fast-triple chorale derived clearly from the Italian *balletto,* a dance-like *a a b b* secular song with fa-la-la refrains (which were transformed into Hallelujahs). The triple time of GELOBT SEI GOTT, 1609 (*MH* 610), creates an energetic, rolling-around effect (see pp. 65-66). WER NUR DEN LIEBEN GOTT, 1641 (*MH* 314), LOBE DEN HERREN, DEN MÄCHTIGEN KÖNIG, 1665 (*MH* 9), and the German Catholic tune, LASST UNS ERFREUEN, 1623 (*MH* 51-52), are further illustrations of a new triple character.

More subtle changes were taking place in the seventeenth-century chorales. Erik Routley describes them in *Music of Christian Hymnody:*

> That operatic style of music, with its emphases on individual prowess and virtuoso technique, on captivating melody and subservient harmony, which began with Peri and Caccini at the beginning of the century, is the chief influence at work to modify, and in the end to overthrow, the traditional conception of the chorale, and to turn it into a song. At the beginning of the period [1615] we see the chorale, under the influence of the Genevan style, growing away from the popular folk-song style into dignified and solemn church style. At the end [1714] it has abandoned that church style for a new kind of secular style associated not with folk-music but with professional music—an altogether new idea.[1]

In 1664, LOBE DEN HERREN, O MEINE SEELE, *MH* 20, appeared for the first time in *Neu-vermehrte Christliche Seelenharpf,* published in Ansbach, accompanying the text "Lobet den Herren aller Herren." The cadence to the end of the *Stollen* was ornamented a bit in operatic style, and it included a vigorous rhythmic feature called *hemiola*: $\frac{3}{4}$ time regroups itself into $\frac{3}{2}$. For example, the first phrase begins in $\frac{3}{4}$ but turns into $\frac{3}{2}$ for the cadence: (The dotted bars are added to the original, Zahn 4994.)

By 1714, when LOBE DEN HERREN was published with the text "Lobe den Herren" for the first time, its rhythm had lost much of its vigor. It was included in the famous collection of Freylinghausen (1670-1739), *Neues Geistreiches Gesangbuch,* Halle, 1714. The 1664, 1714, and 1969 (*MH* 20) versions are here for comparison:

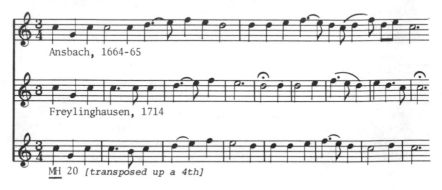

The General Conference Mennonites have used this tune in all of their German books and in the *Mennonite Hymnary,* 1940. *Gesangbuch mit Noten,* 1891, *Gesangbuch,* 1942, and *Mennonite Hymnary,* 1940, all used the Freylingshausen version, which is probably simpler than the Ansbach for congregational use. The Canadian Mennonites in their 1965 *Gesangbuch* adapted the 1665 Ansbach rhythm, which compilers of *The Mennonite Hymnal* in turn borrowed. Choirs might try the hemiola version at the ends of the first, third, fifth, and last lines.[2] The last phrase, for example, would read:

The author of "Lobe den Herren," Johann Daniel Herrnschmidt (1675-1723), spent most of his life in Halle teaching and preaching. Julian commented: "He was one of the best hymn-writers of the older Pietistic school. His hymns are Scriptural, and mirror his inner life, but do not possess much poetic force."[3]

The translator, Lester Hostetler, has also spent most of his life teaching and preaching, though farming and piano tuning are his vocations as well. Lester Hostetler was born in Sugarcreek, Ohio, in 1892. He graduated from Goshen College, Union Theological Seminary, and Oberlin College of Theology. After holding pastorates in Walnut Creek and Sugarcreek, Ohio, he went to the First Mennonite Church in Upland, California. He taught at Bethel College, North Newton, Kansas, and served as pastor for the Bethel College Church. After several years in Freeman, South Dakota, he retired to his orchard and piano tuning in Sugarcreek. From time to time he has commented that his retirement consists of "tuning and pruning, of praying and spraying!" He lives now in Goshen, Indiana.

Hostetler, along with Walter Hohmann, edited the *Mennonite Hymnary,* 1940, for the General Conference Mennonite Church. It was a very strong book that combined the German ethnic background of many of the General Conference Mennonites with representative materials from English and American hymnals. Two distinctive features set it apart from other Mennonite hymnbooks. First, the organization was unique. Distinct types of hymns, such as chorales, gospel songs, and metrical psalms, were placed in separate sections. "Unless our judgment errs, this plan will make them easier to find and more usable than if they were scattered throughout the book according to their subject matter," wrote the editors in their preface (p. v). The first section, Book One— Hymns, was arranged in much the same sequence as the entire *Mennonite Hymnal.* Another significant section was Book Two—Hymns for Children.

The arrangement by styles of music and text rather than subject was a striking departure from the organizational schemes of most hymnals, and it acknowledged the unspoken practice that hymns tend to be selected for their total impact—their ethos. We urge each other to pay attention to the words, "where the meaning lies," but our choices often speak to much more than words.

Many General Conference Mennonites valued this feature. When the compilers of *The Mennonite Hymnal* discussed organization for their joint venture, the question of sectioning by styles naturally emerged. The committee debated the issue for several years. It is hard to imagine in retrospect the intensity of feeling that arose, but the type of organization was the issue that brought the sharpest clashes. The solution was a compromise, achieved—as was the case with every decision—by consensus. There are two sections by type—Gospel Songs and Choral Hymns (meaning here, difficult or suitable for a choir). The rest of the book is arranged by subject.

The second distinctive feature of *The Mennonite Hymnary* was the emphasis on the Church Year. The Book of Chorales emphasized the successive seasons, and the editor's preface presented some educational material, adding this sentence: "The observance of the Church Year has the advantage of giving a well-balanced Christ-centered program of worship and adding variety, color and interest to the church life" (p. vi).

This emphasis on the Church Year was foreign to the Mennonite Church of 1940, but it kept the General Conference Mennonites in contact with German language hymnals and the broad, ecumenical base that had interested them for many years. Their first English hymnal of 1894, *Mennonite Hymnal, A Blending of Many Voices*, was a mainstream Protestant collection, published by A. S. Barnes, to which the name *Mennonite Hymnal* was added and from which one or two hymns on infant baptism were removed.

The *Mennonite Hymnary* was a fine achievement, but Lester Hostetler made an even more remarkable contribution to Mennonites in his *Handbook to the Mennonite Hymnary*, 1949 (Newton, Kansas: General Conference Mennonite Church of North America, see p. 11-12). With a minimum of time at his disposal and a minimum of materials—for example, he listed seven handbooks available to him in contrast to twenty-three we are working with—he and his wife, Charity, produced a book with helpful comments on each hymn. [4]

The *Handbook to the Mennonite Hymnary* opened with "An Introduction to Our Hymns and Tunes, with Illustrations from the *Hymnary*." In nineteen topics within twenty-eight pages he presented a concise history of hymnody (eleven essays), a history of Mennonite hymns and hymnals (2), and single articles on defining a hymn, women hymn writers, practical issues in singing, problems of translating, and John Wesley's rules for singing. Topic number 16, titled "Church Unity in the Hymnbook," pointed to twelve different denominations in this "Mennonite" hymnal and listed contributions from each to the *Hymnary*.

One of the most valuable features of Hostetler's book was the inclusion of all the stanzas of chorales in German. He gives all eight stanzas for "Praise Thou the Lord, O My Soul" at number 513, and says of the English, "The translation here given is a free rendering of stanzas 1 and 8 and was made especially for the *Hymnary*." (That is, the *Mennonite Hymnary*, 1940.) Here are stanzas 1 and 8:

Lobe den Herren, o meine Seele!
    Ich will ihn loben bis zum Tod;
Weil ich noch Stunden auf Erden zähle,
    Will ich lobsingen meinem Gott.
Der Leib und Seel' gegeben hat,
Werde gepriesen früh und spat.
    Halleluja! Halleluja!

Rühmet, ihr Menschen, den hohen Namen
    Des, der so grosse Wunder tut!
Alles, was Odem hat, rufe Amen!

Und bringe Lob mit frohem Mut.
Ihr Kinder Gottes, lobt und preist
Vater und Sohn und Heil'gen Geist!
Halleluja! Halleluja!

Another fine book edited by Lester Hostetler is *The Youth Hymnary,* 1956. Although complete in itself, it supplemented the *Mennonite Hymnary,* 1940, particularly in areas of spirituals, carols, part songs (2- and 3-part treble and soprano-alto-bass), and canons and rounds. A few of the hymns were given descants.

It was logical for Lester Hostetler to be one of the editors of *The Mennonite Hymnal,* along with Walter E. Yoder (see below). He had worked for a time on the committee of *Church Hymnal,* 1927, until, in those troubled days, the committee dissolved and reorganized. He had coedited the *Mennonite Hymnary,* 1940. Thus, he not only brought his expertise to the joint project, but he symbolized the healing of rifts.

[1] Erik Routley, *Music of Christian Hymnody.* London: Independent Press, 1957, p. 69.

[2] *MH* 116 actually incorporates hemiola cadences in the first, second, and last phrases. Alternation between $\frac{3}{4}$ and $\frac{3}{2}$ is the basis for the rhythm of three *Mennonite Hymnal* chorales from this period: *MH* 17, 91, and 481. Numbers 91 and 481 especially can be learned easily by first singing all the notes equal in length, i.e. ♪♪♪♪♪♪♪♪ etc. Then say the rhythm of the words in ♩ and ♪ notes. Finally, sing it as written.

[3] Julian, p. 516.

[4] The accompanying volume of the present series will follow, in abbreviated form, his format in examining each hymn.

438. Teach Me Thy Truth, O Mighty One. GOSHEN.

Walter E. Yoder (1889-1964), coeditor of *The Mennonite Hymnal* with Lester Hostetler, was a Metamora, Illinois, dairy farmer and school-teacher until in 1931 when he moved his family to Goshen College to develop the music department there. He had studied at Goshen College, and he completed his master's degree in music at Northwestern University during his first years of teaching. He was a fine teacher of music theory and director of choirs. His song leading deeply influenced three decades of students and helped many Mennonite Church congregations to sing hymns with joy.

Yoder spent many years studying hymns and occasionally wrote tunes which were incorporated in the Mennonite Church books. His AMAMUS carried a marriage text in the *Church Hymnal,* 1927. Four of his tunes appeared in *Life Songs 2,* 1938. His tune writing reminds me of the tendency of his teacher, J. D. Brunk, to write functional works in varying styles (see pp. 67-68). In his teaching, Yoder urged Mennonites to move beyond gospel songs in their tastes. The fact that THE HOUR OF PRAYER and SILVANUS (*Life Songs 2,* Nos. 67 and 309) are in gospel-song style demonstrates, I believe, his teaching technique of beginning with what people know and like. For although the refrains and frequent repetitions of these two hymns point to the gospel-song tradition, the harmonies are too rich and complex for the style.

GOSHEN (*MH* 438) was one of his four tunes published in *Life Songs 2.* He wrote it for that book after Edith Witmer sent him her text, "Teach Me Thy Truth," to set to music.

Edith Witmer (b. 1902) taught home economics at Goshen College in the late 1920s. Poor health forced her to return to her home in Lancaster, Pennsylvania, where she has lived ever since. She commented on her hymn in an article in the December 4, 1956, issue of *Gospel Herald:*

> It was my conviction while teaching at Goshen College that a Christian college should have in addition to their "Alma Mater" a special college hymn for their worship services. The motto of Goshen College is "Culture for Service." Of course, this was always interpreted to mean Christian service. I had the general idea and the conviction. Then the thoughts, and even the words in rhyme, came quite easily.

Walter Yoder made an excellent bridge from the Mennonite Church hymnals to *The Mennonite Hymnal* through his work on *Songs of the Church,* 1953. In this book of 274 hymns and tunes he included twenty-eight German chorales from the General Conference *Mennonite Hymnary,* 1940, and incorporated several other favorites from that book—for example, THE BEAUTIFUL STREAM (*MH* 556), "O Come Loud Anthems" with SALISBURY (*MH* 14), and DIADEM as the second tune for "All Hail the Power of Jesus' Name" (*MH* 601). He also bridged the gap between the *Church Hymnal* and *Harmonia Sacra,* which was represented by eleven distinctive early American works—folk tunes, set pieces, and anthems. He welcomed Mennonite texts and tunes into the book—eleven tunes and six text-tune combinations.

He included occasional anthems—"Praise God from Whom All Blessings" (*MH* 606)—or pieces more complicated than the standard hymn—"Cast Thy Burden" (*MH* 643), "Christ, We Do All Adore Thee" (*MH* 644), "When All Thy Mercies" (*MH* 74). Had he organized his book by types, he would have had a good section of challenging pieces for choirs, corresponding to *MH* 595 and following.

In short, Walter E. Yoder exerted a strong influence on the character of *The Mennonite Hymnal,* even though his work on the committee was cut short by his death in 1964.

40. I Sing with Exultation.
NUN WEND IHR HÖREN SAGEN.
344. He Who Would Follow Christ.
WARUM BETRÜBST DU DICH, MEIN HERZ.

The Mennonite Hymnal includes three hymns from the *Ausbund*. This hymnbook is important to Mennonites as our earliest collection of texts. The first edition, *Etliche schöne christliche Geseng/wie in der Gefengkniss zu Passaw im Schloss von den Schweitzer Brüdern durch Gottes Gnad geticht und gesungen worden...,* was published in 1564. The book is important also because it is the oldest Protestant hymnal in continuous publication and still used today. To commemorate its four-hundreth year, Herald Press (Scottdale, Pennsylvania) issued a 48-page history, called *Four Hundred Years with the Ausbund,* 1964.[1]

The nucleus of the *Ausbund* consisted of fifty-one hymns written by Anabaptists who were imprisoned in the dungeons of the castle of Passau on the Danube River in Bavaria between 1537 and 1540. The second edition, 1583, incorporated eighty new hymns. A few hymns were removed through the various editions and a few added. The thirteenth edition, 1935, which is still being reprinted, has 140 hymns in 895 four-by-six inch pages.

Elizabeth Bender summarized the contents of the *Ausbund* thus: "ballad-like poems recounting the sufferings, the testimony, and the death of the Anabaptist martyrs ... hymns of faith and worship written by martyrs and other persons, and perhaps a dozen hymns of non-Anabaptist origin."[2] The hymns often accept the general faith of Protestants, but they reveal unique Anabaptist beliefs as well—on baptism, on nonviolence, on the inevitability of persecution and yearning for the New Jerusalem.[3]

No edition includes tunes, but at the head of each hymn the name of an appropriate tune or two appears. Rosella Reimer Duerksen, who made a thorough study of the tunes,[4] points out that, although these melodic designations are valuable, they do not tell us the specific form of the tune; they sometimes indicate interchangeable tunes in the same meter. She finds seventy-three different tune designations out of 130 hymns. Of these "a total of 41 *Ausbund* tunes—over one-half—are duplicates of tunes used among the Moravian Anabaptists, or Hutterites."[5]

When Duerksen traced the sources of tunes, she found Anabaptists borrowing occasionally from the Roman Catholics. The favorite of these tunes was PANGE LINGUA which was linked with passion texts. We included this chant in *MH* 404 primarily because of its Anabaptist use. Some tune names pointed to pre-Reformation sacred tunes, others to secular folk melodies. Anabaptists borrowed freely from German

Protestants and, in rare cases, from French Calvinists. Duerksen suggests that perhaps the titles which could not be identified might have been the Anabaptists' own compositions, but there is no way to know definitely.[6]

Two of the three *Mennonite Hymnal* hymns from the *Ausbund* appeared in the first edition—*MH* 40 and 344. Here is a summary of their characteristics:

MH 40 and 344 have in common:	*Specific Details:* *MH* 40	*MH* 344
Texts are by or about a martyr of the 1520s	Felix Manz, d. 1527	Jörg Wagner, d. 1527
Many ballad-like stanzas	18	27
Use a brief selection in *MH*	St. 1, 2, 7, 9,	Compilation of st. 1-5
Organization in lines and meters —Original —Translation	7 lines: 7.5.7.5.8.7.6. 8 lines: 7.5.7.5.7.6.7.6.	5 lines: 8.8.7.8.7. 5 lines: 8.8.6.8.6.
Observe a rhyme scheme —Original —Translation	a b a b c d c a b c b d e f e	a a b c b a a b c b
Tune suggested in *Ausbund*. (Secular in both cases)	"Ich stund an einem Morgen"	"Wiewohl ich jeztz ganz elend bin" (& another)
Tune Details Tune chosen for *MH*	NUN WEND IHR HÖREN SAGEN	WARUM BETRÜBST DU DICH, MEIN HERZ
Source for *MH* tune	*Benzenaur Ton,* 1504 in Bäumker,[7] no. 26, pp. 267-8 vol. 1	Manuscript of Bartholomeus Monoetius, 1565 in Zahn 1689a

"I Sing with Exultation" (*MH* 40) was written by Felix Manz (c. 1498-1527), one of the founders and first martyrs of the Swiss Brethren congregation in Zürich.[8] He followed Zwingli's teaching for several years but broke with him in 1524 on issues of adult baptism and communion. After a series of disputations and imprisonments he was drowned in Lake Zürich in January of 1527, saying at the moment of his death, "Into thy hands I commend my spirit."

Marion Wenger (b. 1932), Professor of German at Goshen College, chose to translate the text by using a German folk tune as his metrical framework rather than adhering strictly to the original meter. The tune he chose, DIE BLÜMLELEIN SIE SCHLAFEN, had an appropriate meter for the text—7.5.7.5.8.6.6. It began:

The principle of choosing a folk tune was appropriate and his melody, singable. However, the compilers decided instead to use a sixteenth-century melody which was suggested to be used with a hymn by Jörg Wagner, *Ausbund* number 34.[9] The melody, "Im Bentzenhauer Ton," which was one of three soldier tunes, recalled a battle at Kufstein in 1504.[10] The year 1540 is probably an error in *The Mennonite Hymnal*.

Attributing the hymn "He Who Would Follow Christ" (*MH* 344) to Jörg Wagner is a serious error, for which I take responsibility. The hymn is not *by* Wagner but *about* him. David Augsburger, the translator, had annotated his translation as follows:

He who would Follow Christ

Ausbund 11

Anonymous Hymn Commemorating martyrdom

of Georg Wagner (d. 1527)

(Translated and compiled from stanzas 1 to 5)

The second stanza reads:

Also thät Jörg der Wagner auch,
Gen Himmel fuhr er in dem Rauch,
  Durchs Creutz ward er bewähret,
Gleich wie man thut dem klaren Gold,
  Von Herzen ers begehret.

The third stanza refers to the Falkenturm (in Bavaria) where he was tortured. Details of his life continue to recur through the twenty-seven stanzas. Augsburger paraphrased the poem so that it represents the martyr in general rather than Wagner in particular.

Jörg Wagner's religious affiliation is not clear. H. S. Bender said that he was not an Anabaptist but that he was a martyr claimed by both Anabaptists and Lutherans.[11] His beliefs—that priests cannot forgive sin, that God is not bodily in the bread, that a human cannot bring God from heaven, and that the water of baptism does not save—led to his imprisonment, torture, and eventual burning on February 8, 1527.

David Augsburger (b. 1938), who is professor of pastoral care at the Associated Mennonite Biblical Seminaries in Elkhart, Indiana, preferred that a tune be chosen which is immediately accessible to a congregation. Once again, as with *MH* 40, the compilers selected a tune on a historical rather than practical basis. WARUM BETRÜBST DU DICH, MEIN HERZ comes from the decade of the *Ausbund's* first edition. The tune had appeared in the major mode for two secular songs in 1560 (Zahn 1689b), and Zahn claims that it surely must have existed in earlier secular uses.

WARUM BETRÜBST DU DICH is difficult chiefly because it begins with half notes (♩) and subdivides into quarters (♪) from the third phrase to the end. Thus, choosing a reasonable tempo is crucial; it is easy to begin too rapidly for the quick notes and chord changes of the last half.

[1] *Four Hundred Years with the Ausbund.* Scottdale, Pa.: Herald Press, 1964.

[2] *Ibid.,* p. 19.

[3] *Ibid.,* p. 23.

[4] "Anabaptist Hymnody in the sixteenth century" (Ph.D. dissertation, Union Theological Seminary, 1956); see also Rupert K. Hohmann, "The Church Music of the Old Order Amish of the United States" (Ph.D. dissertation, Northwestern University, 1959), and Charles Burkhart, "The Music of the Old Order Amish and the Old Colony Mennonites: A Contemporary Monodic Practice" (M.A. thesis, Colorado College, 1952).

[5] Summary of Duerksen, pp. 81-2.

[6] *Ibid.,* pp. 83-134. See also Johann Peter Classen, "Handbuch zum Ausbund der Alten Täuffer," Winnipeg, Manitoba 1944-56. (Mennonite Heritage Centre, Winnipeg, Man.).

[7] W. Bäumker, *Das Katholische deutsche Kirchen lied in seinen Singweisen.* Hildesheim: Georg Olms, 1962, pp. 267-8.

[8] For more information, see "Manz, Felix," *Mennonite Encyclopedia,* III:472-74, C. Neff and H. S. Bender.

[9] The Canadian *Gesangbuch der Mennoniten,* 1965, used the *Ausbund* text and tune at number 594.

[10] From Johannes Kulp, *Handbuch zum Evangelischen Kirchengesangbuch.* Gottingen: Vandenhoeck & Ruprecht, 1958, pp. 312-13.

[11] "Wagner, Georg," *Mennonite Encyclopedia,* IV:869, H. S. Bender.

384. Our Father God Thy Name.
NUN FREUT EUCH.

"Our Father God, Thy Name We Praise" (*MH* 384) is the most frequently used of the three Anabaptist hymns in *The Mennonite Hymnal.* It is the second hymn in every Amish service.[1] Its author was Leenaerdt Clock (or Klock), a Mennonite preacher who moved from Germany to Holland around 1590. He was a prolific writer of devotional hymns, often written in acrostics. His "O Gott Vater" appeared at page 669 in the seventeenth-century, first edition of the *Ausbund.* We know that he was still active in 1625 when he published *A Formulary of Several*

Christian Prayers. Otherwise dates for his life are not known.

The translator, Ernest A. Payne (1902-1980) was an English Baptist minister, leader in Baptist circles, and former president of the World Council of Churches (1968-75). William J. Reynolds reports in the *Companion to Baptist Hymnal:*

> In 1950, while visiting in Goshen, Indiana, Ernest A. Payne found a copy of the *Ausbund* in a bookstore. Six years later, he made the English translation ["Our Father God"] for use in a lecture he gave to the Congregational Historical Society. In 1962 it was published in the *British Baptist Hymn Book.* [2]

Only three stanzas (*MH* 1, 2, and 4) were used in the British book. However, the printed lecture mentioned above, "The First Free Church Hymnal (1583)," included stanza 3, which Dr. Payne graciously consented to let us use, even though he felt that the three stanzas made a cohesive unit without the fourth.

The tune suggested in the *Ausbund* is AUS TIEFER NOT. There were two tunes for that text published in the 1520s. The first was a fine, but difficult, melody in the Phrygian mode (E to E on the white keys of the piano), published in 1524:

Zahn 4437   etc.

AUS TIEFER NOT (*MH* 234), 1525, (see p. 118) would have been possible, but we chose a tune from 1535—NUN FREUTEUCH (see p. 105). Walter E. Yoder, coeditor of *The Mennonite Hymnal,* remembered hearing NUN FREUTEUCH among Indiana Amish, and we expected it to be usable for congregational singing.

The Amish singing of "O Gott Vater," which they call *'s Lobg'sang,* reveals a remarkable oral tradition which interests musicologists and folklorists. It is a very slow, [3] embellished style. George Pullen Jackson, who in all his work searched for connections with previously existing music, speculated that the extremely slow singing could not retain sustained sounds without changing, and that ornaments entered unwittingly. He was convinced that the skeleton of the melody, when embellishments were removed, was an identifiable sixteenth-century tune. [4]

Charles Burkhart (see p. 116 footnote) made transcriptions of three recordings of "O Gott Vater" from different groups of Amish. These he added to the transcription published by Joseph W. Yoder in 1942 [5] in the table of comparisons below (Table 2). The ornamental first phrase of each version is shown. He introduced his transcriptions as follows:

Like any musical style, or any performance practice, that of the Amish (and the Old Colonists as well) cannot be fully apprehended without a hearing of the music itself. The temporal element of this style cannot even be notated in our present system. To facilitate his task, therefore, the writer took the liberty of superimposing a beat on the Amish tunes, but since the Amish themselves feel no regular meter, a strict beat should definitely not be preserved in singing the transcriptions. In some case, where the metrical notation was particularly inadequate, a horizontal line was placed over certain notes to indicate that they are to be lengthened. The writer makes no claims to complete accuracy in his transcription of both rhythm and ornamentation.[6]

Rupert Hohmann developed further Jackson's technique of extracting the skeleton or "root" melody from the Amish tune (p. 116, footnote). He discovered that the root melody is indeed AUS TIEFER NOT—the 1525 version. His transcription of a version from Partridge, Kansas, is at 5a and the root melody, 5b. (Compare 5b with *MH* 234, first phrase.)

Table 2

SOURCES: Lines 1-4. Burkhart, p. 94.
Lines 5a and 5b. Hohmann, p. 234.
Line 6. Olen Yoder, No. 1.

The sixth version[7] comes from a publication of an Amishman, Olen Yoder, who prepared a collection of thirty-nine tunes for eighty-one texts of the *Ausbund,* to be used at singing rehearsals. Yoder gave the pitches but made no attempt to show rhythm. Nevertheless, this type of notation is a great help to the young Amish who want to learn and retain the traditional tunes. The use of notes is most unusual. The slow singing is an oral tradition which results in many variations from one locality or generation to another, as these transcriptions show.

[1] Amish worship is more liturgical than is Mennonite worship in its emphasis on a prescribed form and contents. "Scriptures read at the Amish preachings follow a seasonal pattern. The register of Scriptures begins at Christmas time with the birth of Christ and concludes with the New Testament account of the judgment and end of the world. There are Scripture selections for sowing and harvesting. Selections from the hymnal (*Ausbund*) are integrated with the register of Scripture and hymns." (John A. Hostetler, *Amish Society,* Baltimore: Johns Hopkins, 1963, pp. 113-14.)

[2] William J. Reynolds, *Companion to Baptist Hymnal.* Nashville: Broadman Press, 1976, p. 177.

[3] "To sing all four verses takes twenty minutes in some of the most conservative Amish communities, while in some places it is sung in eleven minutes. Amish music reflects culture, and the speed of singing can be positively correlated with a degree of assimilation." (Hostetler, p. 125.)

[4] "The Strange Music of the Old Order Amish," *Music Quarterly,* 21 (July, 1945), 275-88.

[5] Huntingdon, Pa: The Yoder Publishing Co.

[6] Burkhart transcription, pp. 51-2.

[7] No title. Goshen, Indiana, n.d.

199. Wake the Song of Jubilee. AMBOY.

"Wake the Song of Jubilee" is one of three mission hymns by Leonard Bacon (1802-81) which he brought out in his tract, *Hymns and Sacred Songs for the Monthly Concert,* 1823. This collection "was the earliest American attempt to provide hymns giving utterance to the fervor for missions which was sweeping the evangelical bodies."[1]

Bacon knew one area of mission work intimately. His father was a Congregational missionary to the Indians in Detroit, where Leonard was born. His active promotion of missions and his involvement in social concerns led Charles Robinson to say of him after his death: "His face was a part of every photograph of the American Board of Foreign Missions. His voice rang in every debate which disrupted the Tract Society. For he was early in the antislavery agitation and was a tremendous orator on a platform."[2]

To my knowledge no current hymnal besides *The Mennonite Hymnal* uses either "Wake the Song" or AMBOY. In recent years the combination was introduced to Mennonites in *Songs of the Church,* 1953, from *Harmonia Sacra,* where it was first printed in the sixth edition, 1854. Funk may have found it in *The Psaltery: a New Collection of Church Music,* published first in 1845, or in one of the many editions which followed. Incidentally, AMBOY is printed in the 1845 edition with the melody in the tenor, and with a note at the top indicating, "Treble and Tenor may be inverted." Lowell Mason and his brother, Timothy, had published the *Ohio Sacred Harp* in the 1830s in which they said of the treble or leading melody, "This part is always to be sung by female voices, and by them alone."[3] (See page 124 for a fuller comment on this practice.)

In spite of Lowell Mason's urging that the soprano take the melody, his tunes sound good in my ears as printed originally, with the melody in the tenor. Try AMBOY or ANTIOCH (*MH* 122) with soprano and tenor reversing parts.

Lowell Mason (1792-1872) was born into a family active in music and education. Except for fifteen years in Savannah, Georgia, his life was spent in Massachusetts. He was a banker for a time in both Savannah and Boston, but he is known primarily for his work in music.[4]

Mason's determination to educate young children led eventually to the establishment of public school music in Boston. He helped to found the Boston Academy of Music, which was active from 1833 to 1847. He encouraged a high level of musical performance, both through his directing of choirs and through his critical writings on performances he heard in Europe. Typical of his observations is the following letter from Edinburgh, March 26, 1853, in which he commented on the state of Scottish church music:

> [One] reason for the low state of church-music in Scotland may be found in the absence of organs. Choirs and organs are both necessary, not only to the greatest success of church-music, but also to the best syle of Congregational singing.[5]

He made visits to Europe in 1837 and 1852-53, where he heard concerts of Schumann and Mendelssohn, among others.

Lowell Mason published a continuous stream of anthologies of music, beginning in 1822 with *Boston Handel and Haydn Society Collection of Church Music* (see p. 57) and carrying on into the 1860s. Many of his books, such as *The Boston Academy's Collection of Church Music, Carmina Sacra, The Psaltery,* and *The Song-book of the School-room,* were revised and reissued almost annually.[6]

Many of the works were his own compositions or arrangements. Henry L. Mason reported that Lowell Mason produced a total of 1,697 tunes—1,210 of his own and 487 arrangements or adaptations from many sources.[7] The arrangements, however, are often not traceable to the suggested source. ANTIOCH, for example, which Lowell Mason identified as "From Handel" has only the sketchiest relationship to any Handel work discovered thus far.[8]

The Mennonite Hymnal includes more tunes by Mason than by any other composer-arranger—twenty-seven in all, several of which are used more than once. A few are linked strongly with a given text in many hymnals—ANTIOCH (*MH* 122), HAMBURG (*MH* 167), OLIVET (*MH* 251), BETHANY (*MH* 289), and DENNIS (*MH* 385). Others function as common tunes—AZMON (*MH* 104), NAOMI (*MH* 213), EVAN (*MH* 259), BOYLSTON (*MH* 350). Psalm meters (L.M., C.M., S.M.) represent slightly over half of the tunes in *The Mennonite Hymnal*; nine other meters are present. Some tunes are fairly sedate and calm—NAOMI and OLIVET, for example. Others like HARWELL (*MH* 201) and GERAR (*MH* 382), bounce along with dotted rhythms. Frequently one rhythm pattern, such as ♩♪♪♩♩♪♪♩, dominates, as in AZMON, NASHVILLE (*MH* 25), and ROCKINGHAM NEW (*MH* 398).

Gilbert Chase's perspective on Mason is helpful. The nineteenth century, he says, stood for progress through science, and valued words like *good taste* and *correctness*. Mason's tastes were dominated by Europe. He arranged music of European masters, looked to Europe for appropriate performance practices, and found in Europe his methods for teaching music. Thus, genuinely American styles and practices—imitation, fuging, revival spirituals, folk hymns, shape notes, and melody sung by tenors—seemed to him crude. One can see the gradual change toward his views in successive editions of his popular publications. "He was instrumental in thrusting the native American tradition . . . into the background while opening the gates for a flood of colorless imitations of the 'European masters.' "[9]

A similar process took place in the compiling of Mennonite hymnals. In trying to choose the tune for "How Firm a Foundation" (*MH* 260 and 261) the committee weighed two possibilities—the European ADESTE FIDELES and the American folk tune BELLEVUE or FOUNDATION (which appeared for the first time in print in Funk's *Genuine Church Music,* 1832). Chester Lehman, who had been a member of the committee for the 1927 *Church Hymnal,* recalled that his committee had dropped the folk tune in favor of the European, ADESTE FIDELES, because the church had "advanced far enough educationally" to do so. The opinions in our committee (1960s) were so mixed that we accepted both the folk tune and the "better music" for *The Mennonite Hymnal.*

AMBOY is in some ways a bland imitation of its European models. For example, its chords have a more limited range of tension and resolution than many European tunes of the mid-nineteenth century. (See *MH* 5, 16, 43, 174, 191, 279, 347 for comparison with AMBOY.) Its melody and rhythm are simple and repetitious. But AMBOY "works" in congregational singing. It supports its text exuberantly.

[1] Henry Wilder Foote, *Three Centuries of American Hymnody*. Cambridge: Harvard University Press, 1940, p. 214.

[2] *Annotations upon Popular Hymns*. New York: Hunt and Eaton 1893, p. 489.

[3] Quoted in Jackson, *White Spirituals . . .* , p. 18.

[4] For a concise biography see *Guide to the Pilgrim Hymnal* by Ronander and Porter. Philadelphia: United Church Press, 1966, pp. 206-7.

[5] Lowell Mason, *Musical Letters from Abroad,* 1854. Reprint, New York: Da Capo Press, 1967, pp. 311-12.

[6] The J. D. Hartzler collection (see p. 102) has thirty-four Mason titles and seventy distinct editions. The *Boston Handel and Haydn Society Collection . . .* , for example, is represented by eight different editions, from 1822 to 1834.

[7] *Hymn-Tunes of Lowell Mason*. Cambridge: Harvard University Press, 1944, p. vi.

[8] See William J. Reynolds, *Companion to Baptist Hymnal*. Nashville: Broadman Press, 1976, p. 128.

[9] *America's Music*. New York: McGraw-Hill, 1955, p. 160.

74. When All Thy Mercies, O My God. GENEVA.

Joseph Addison (1672-1719), along with Richard Steele, began publishing the daily *Spectator* in London in 1711 to "enliven morality with wit, and to temper wit with morality." In the August 9, 1912, issue Addison had an essay on "Gratitude" followed by the hymn "When All Thy Mercies." The Methodist *Companion to the Hymnal* quotes from that essay:

There is not a more pleasing exercise of the mind than gratitude. It is accompanied with such an inward satisfaction, that the duty is sufficiently rewarded by the performance. It is not like the practice of many other virtues, difficult and painful, but attended with so much pleasure, that were there no positive command which enjoined it, nor any recompense laid up for it hereafter, a generous mind would indulge in it, for the natural gratification that accompanies it. If gratitude is due from man to man, how much more from man to his Maker. [1]

The hymn is in thirteen stanzas, of which 1, 10, 11, and 13 are in *The Mennonite Hymnal*. It must have enjoyed a wide use, because even though it was not a psalm, it was included in the 1718 printing of Tate and Brady's *New Version,* and it was one of only five hymns appended to the *Scottish Paraphrases* of 1781. Incidentally, across the page from "When All Thy Mercies" was "The Spacious Firmament on High" (*MH* 56) which had been published in the *Spectator* on August 23, 1712.

The tune, GENEVA, at *MH* 74, is not, as one might suspect, a Genevan psalm tune. Instead it is an American imitative piece. It is not the usual fuging tune (see pp. 99-100) because it begins with imitation rather than introducing it near the center. It is not long enough to be called an anthem, which EASTER ANTHEM (*MH* 613) and DEDICATION ANTHEM (*MH* 606) illustrate very well. GENEVA seems to be a tune influenced by the ornate European style of William Tans'ur (c. 1706-83), an English singing master whose works were reprinted and sung in the Colonies. The dotted rhythms of his ST. MARTIN'S (*MH* 109) are echoed in the last half of GENEVA.

The first appearance I have found of GENEVA is in *Ecclesiastical Harmony, a Collection of Ancient and Modern Tunes Particularly Adapted to Dr. Dwight's [2] Collection of Psalms and Hymns; including a number never before published in this country* by John Cole in 1805.

GENEVA appeared with John Cole's name in three voices; beginning with:

In that same year, 1805, Cole's *The Beauties of Harmony* included GENEVA in four voices with the text "When All Thy Mercies"—all thirteen stanzas:

Episcopalian Harmony of 1811 published it again in four parts. Cole's "Prefatory Remarks" reveal much about performance practice and clashes of taste in his day. He identified himself as a "clerk and Teacher of Psalmody" in the Protestant Episcopal Church and stated his interest in publishing for that church. Then he continued,

The editor would earnestly recommend that in all regular choirs, schools or societies where this work may be introduced, the Air or principal melody be performed by the treble voices. In this arrangement, which prevails in all regular performances in Europe, and is now happily becoming more and more prevalent among us, there is no unmeaning jumble of sounds; for the acuteness of the treble voices renders the Air predominant, and the music becomes intelligible even to those acquainted with the nature of Harmony.

The editors of THE MONTHLY ANTHOLOGY, speaking on this head, observe, that "The principal Air is the soul of the piece—it ought to be more distinctly heard, and its effect should be heightened as much as possible by the auxiliary efforts of the other parts—giving the character to the piece it ought to be placed in the most conspicuous station, and assigned to those voices which are naturally the most expressive of melody . . . Good treble voices exceed, on a moderate calculation, the number of good tenor voices in the proportion of twenty to one. On account, therefore, of the superior delicacy of the female voice, and of the greater number of the treble performers, to them ought to be assigned the principal Air of the piece. Owing to the general deficiency in musical science, which characterizes American masters, and to the almost total want of refinement in the public ear, the ancient practice of giving the Air to the tenor, and casting the treble voices into the shade, still prevails.

Cole's distaste for American music, presumably folk hymns and revival spirituals, comes through further in his description of his work, *Episcoplian Harmony:*

It does not contain certain tunes which have been bandied about from Maine to Georgia for the last twenty years, to the great annoyance of persons of taste and the regret of all serious worshipers—this trash has had its day, and it is time for us to retrace our steps until we arrive at the true sublime of Psalmody, which is only to be found in the admirable compositions of the great masters of the 14th and 15th centuries.[3]

In *Union Harmony or Music Made Easy,* published around 1829, Cole included his GENEVA again but this time with parts arranged as he wanted them sung, that is, with the melody in the top voice as it appears at *MH* 74. He also marked the third phrase *piano* and the last, *forte,* and set the music in shape notes.

The annotations on the tune are imprecise at *MH* 74. "Version from Joseph Funk's *Harmonia Sacra*" could be any edition from the twelfth, 1867, to the present, twenty-third edition, 1973, published by the Trissels

Mennonite Church, Broadway, Virginia—the church with which the Funk family was associated in Joseph's day. But the actual practice of singing was used rather than the notes themselves, that is, exchanging the soprano and tenor parts. Thus GENEVA's form is virtually that of Cole's 1829 edition, with a few interesting differences.

[1] Gealy, Lovelace, and Young. Nashville: Abingdon, 1970, pp. 429-30.

[2] Timothy Dwight, the president of Yale College and the author of "I Love Thy Kingdom, Lord," 1800 (*MH* 380), had published in 1801 *The Psalms of David by I. Watts. A New edition, in which the Psalms, omitted by Dr. Watts* [see p. 59] *are versified anew* . . . Hartford. The work, generally called *Dwight's Watts* was approved in 1802 by the General Assembly of the Presbyterian Church and remained in heavy use for the first third of the century.

[3] "Prefatory Remarks," n.p.

606. Praise God from Whom All Blessings Flow. DOXOLOGY (DEDICATION ANTHEM).

This series of essays ends, as does many a hymn sing, with *MH* 606. The text, "Praise God from Whom All Blessings Flow," is the doxology which concludes a morning and an evening hymn written by Thomas Ken (1637-1711) around 1700. These are long poems of which we have a few stanzas at *MH* 485 and 496. The music of *MH* 606 is more elaborate than the usual hymn or psalm tune and should probably be called an *anthem.*

William Billings (1746-1800) was the most famous of early-American anthem composers and provided models for the type. His EASTER ANTHEM (*MH* 613) consists of fragments of texts from the Bible and from a long poem by Edward Young (1685-1765)—*The Complaint, and the Consolation: or, Night Thoughts,* from the 1740s. The music is through-composed rather than strophic (strophic uses the same music for each stanza) in order to fit the poem's irregular meter and its meaning. Individual parts often sing alone (as at the beginning), in duets with a contrasting voice (bottom of the first page), or in a fuging arrangement (top of second page, on "And did He rise?" See above, p. 99). Four parts used simultaneously often form an emphatic summary to duet statements, as at the end of the anthem. The effect is somewhat fragmentary, but the scope of the emotion is broader than that of a hymn tune.

Billings said of the imitative aspect of the style: *Imitation* comes "when one part imitates or mimicks another . . . This is frequently done in Fuging pieces."

125

Although Lowell Mason preferred European musical styles, he included *MH* 606, "Praise God from Whom All Blessings Flow," in the ninth edition of *The Boston Handel and Haydn Society Collection of Church Music,* 1830. That is the first appearance I have been able to find, even though 1830 seems a bit late for an anthem of this sort. There, on page 338, after the title, [DOXOLOGY] is printed. For some reason the title DEDICATION ANTHEM has always accompanied the piece in *Harmonia Sacra,* where it first appeared in the fifteenth edition, 1876. The melody is in the tenor and the bass has figures for chords, perhaps implying a keyboard accompaniment.

In the preface, Mason described Maelzel's invention of the metronome. It is valuable, he said, because composers can now show in a simple and decisive manner the speed of their pieces. It also helps the young to be correct and precise in keeping the tempo. "Many of the most respectable composers in Europe, now mark their compositions, by this Metronome" (p. v). He marked "Praise God . . ." ♩ = 100, or 100 quarter notes in one minute. The triple section, which in his edition is $\frac{3}{4}$ rather than $\frac{3}{2}$ (♪♪|♩♩♪♪|♩♩ etc.), is also ♩ = 100, thus signaling a very lively ending.

No composer's name is given. However, in a footnote to the eleventh edition of *The Boston Handel and Haydn Society Collection* . . . , 1831, Mason said, "For this very popular piece the editor acknowledges his obligations to Mr. James Sharp." "Possibly Samuel Stanley, d. 1822" appears in *The Mennonite Hymnal* because it is attributed to Stanley in a copy of the *Harmonia Sacra,* 1876, which belonged to J. H. Hall, a friend of the children of Joseph Funk.[1] Perhaps someone will discover who the composer was by the time Mennonites publish another hymnal.

In the meantime, in spite of the anonymity of the composer, the DOXOLOGY anthem is a "very popular piece," as it was in Lowell Mason's day. Its use has been so widespread in the 1970s that *MH* 606 can almost be called "the Mennonite hymn." Using a basic text, appropriate at any time, the anthem provides a musical vehicle which repeats the text in order to give us varied facets of the words. The "Alleluia-Amen" conclusion carries us beyond the realm of words to exuberant and joyous praise.

---

[1] This copy may be seen in the Eastern Mennonite College Historical Library.

General Index

106n, 116n

133

137

Index of Hymns

587	76		609	54
588	65, 76		610	19, 107
589	76		611	17, 54, 105
595	34		613	101, 123, 125
597	17, 51, 54, 72, 105		616	71
599	54		618	30-32
600	54		632	103
601	112		638	29
603	51		639	29
604	51		643	112
606	101, 112, 123, 125-26		644	112
607	34		645	44